C FOR ROOKIES

Paul J. Perry
Clayton Walnum

C for Rookies

Copyright © 1993 by Que® Corporation

Library of Congress Catalog No.: 93-60617

ISBN: 1-56529-280-4

95 94 93   6 5 4 3 2 1

Interpretation of the printing code: the rightmost double-digit number is the year of the book's printing; the rightmost single-digit number, the number of the book's printing. For example, a printing code of 93-1 shows that the first printing of the book occurred in 1993.

Screen reproductions in this book were created with Collage Plus from Inner Media, Inc., Hollis, NH.

Publisher: David P. Ewing

Associate Publisher: Rick Ranucci

Operations Manager: Sheila Cunningham

Publishing Plan Manager: Thomas H. Bennett

Marketing Manager: Ray Robinson

Dedication

To my parents, thanks for always being there.

Credits

Publishing Manager
Joseph B. Wikert

Acquisitions Editor
Sherri Morningstar

Production Editor
Michael Cunningham

Editors
Lori Cates
Kezia Endsley
Bryan Gambrel
Jodi Jensen
Phil Kitchel

Technical Reviewers
Discovery Computing Inc.
Greg Guntle

Illustrator
Gary Varvel

Book Designer
Amy Peppler-Adams

Production Team
Danielle Bird
Julie Brown
Jodi Cantwell
Paula Carroll
Laurie Casey
Brook Farling
Michelle Greenwalt
Carla Hall-Batton
Heather Kaufman
Bob LaRoche
Caroline Roop
Linda Seifert
Sandra Shay
Amy Steed
Tina Trettin

Composed in Goudy and MCPdigital by Que Corportion

About the Author

Paul J. Perry is a California native and a graduate of California State University, Chico. He started programming in the early days of personal computers when he designed and wrote software in BASIC on early PET computers. Currently he works at a major software company supporting C and C++ as well as writing books on computer programming. Mr. Perry has been programming in C for over five years. He is the author of *Do It Yourself Turbo C++* (Sams Publishing, 1992), and *Crash Course in C* (Que, 1993), as well as a number of other computer books on various topics.

C FOR ROOKIES

Acknowledgments

I would like to thank Joe Wikert for his helpfulness and Michael Cunningham for a great edit job, as well as all the other people behind the scenes at Que.

Trademark Acknowledgments

All terms mentioned in this book that are known to be trademarks or service marks have been appropriately capitalized. Que Corporation cannot attest to the accuracy of this information. Use of a term in this book should not be regarded as affecting the validity of any trademark or service mark.

IBM is a registered trademark of International Business Machines, Inc. MS-DOS is a registered trademark of Microsoft Corporation.

Contents at a Glance

Table of Contents

C FOR ROOKIES

Introduction

Have you ever wondered what goes on inside a computer program? Did you ever want to sit down at your keyboard and conjure up digital magic on your computer's screen? If so, there may be a computer programmer somewhere inside you, screaming to get out.

Unfortunately, you may have found computer programming not only intimidating but downright scary. Heck, you get new gray hairs every time you try to write a simple batch file, right? If you feel this way, *C for Rookies* is here to prove that programming your computer can be fun, rewarding, and—best of all—easy.

Who This Book Is For

This book is for anyone who wants to learn to program their computer with C. More importantly, this book is for anyone who's flipped through other programming texts only to be discouraged by obtuse language, jargon-ridden prose, and stuffed-shirt attitudes. The conversational style you'll find in C *for Rookies* incorporates plain-English explanations along with short programming examples. Together, these elements lead you (the novice programmer) by the hand through the techno-jungle of computer programming.

Because it focuses on beginning programmers, C *for Rookies* is not a complete C reference, nor is it a comprehensive tutorial in the techniques of professional programming. It is meant to give you a quick taste of C programming so that you can decide whether programming is as interesting as you thought it would be. By the end of the book, you will know all you need to write many useful and rewarding programs. After you've worked your way through this entire book, however, you'll probably want to purchase a more advanced text to learn the complete C language. Recommended books are provided at the end of Chapter 9, "Modular Programming."

Software and Hardware Requirements

Although C runs on most IBM-compatible computers that have DOS 5.0 or later, a couple programs in this book require a color monitor. Even if you don't have a color monitor, you can still follow most lessons with little difficulty. In addition, a mouse is often helpful for selecting menus and buttons. But if you don't have a mouse, don't worry. You can control C completely from the keyboard, and you can get by just fine without a mouse. Finally, you must have at least one floppy drive; a hard drive, however, will make your programming much more enjoyable.

As for software, this book comes bundled with a C compiler, called the Personal C Compiler (PCC for short), as well as a full-featured programmer's editor, called Turbo Edit. The rest of the software you'll write yourself!

An Overview of the Book

C for Rookies is composed of nine chapters, each of which concentrates on specific topics of importance to novice programmers. Here's a brief outline of the book:

▼ *Chapter 1* is a brief introduction to the art of programming. Here, you learn what programs are and how they work. You also learn the general programming process.

▼ *Chapter 2* teaches you how to use the Personal C programming environment. You get hands-on experience with Turbo Edit's editor, menus, dialog boxes, and much more.

▼ *Chapter 3* covers such topics as input, output, and variables. You also learn what interactive programs are and how to write them.

▼ *Chapter 4* introduces you to computer mathematics. You learn to do such things as count in a program and write simple C formulas. You also get a quick look at data types.

▼ *Chapter 5* offers a discussion of text in computer programs, including using string (text) variables in conjunction with some of C's most-used string-handling functions.

▼ *Chapter 6* teaches you how computers make decisions. Here, you learn about `if` statements, as well as relational operators (such as greater-than, less-than, and equal-to) and logical operators (`AND`, `OR`, and `NOT`).

▼ *Chapter* 7 introduces you to C's powerful looping constructs, including `for`, `while`, and `do-while` loops. You can use loops to more easily write programs that perform repetitive operations.

▼ *Chapter* 8 teaches you about arrays—special data structures that can hold many values. You'll learn to create numerical and text arrays, as well as discover various ways to load values into an array.

▼ *Chapter* 9 sums up things with a discussion of modular program design.

Conventions Used in This Book

To get the most out of this book, you should know a little about how it's designed. Here are a few tips:

▼ New terms and emphasized words are presented in *italicized text*; pay close attention to these terms. C's keywords, commands, variable names, and the like are set in a special `monospace` type, as in `printf("Hello!")`.

▼ Anything you are asked to type appears in **bold**. Responses to program prompts appear in `monospace bold`.

▼ C programs are numbered and have bold headings, such as **Listing 7.1. REPEAT.C prints your name six times**.

▼ Tables and figures are also numbered and help organize material within chapters.

▼ Descriptive labels, called *callouts*, appear next to some program lines. These callouts help you follow along by pointing to particular items that are being discussed in the text.

What Are Those Drawings in the Margin?

This book uses icons (those funny drawings in the margin) to say things like "Be careful when you do this," or "Here's more information about this new term." The following is an explanation of these visual pointers:

CAUTION

Beware! Warning! This icon warns you of problem areas, including possible cases in which you might introduce bugs into your program or crash your system.

NOTE

This icon points out extraneous information. Sometimes, this information helps speed your learning process and provides you with C shortcuts. Other times, it simply reminds you of information important enough to be mentioned twice.

BUZZWORD

Terms you are being introduced to for the first time are indicated by this icon. These terms often are also italicized in text, but the Buzzword box emphasizes the importance of certain terms. Although C *for Rookies* avoids computer jargon as much as possible, there are some terms that every programmer must understand.

TIP

This icon focuses your attention on suggestions that can help you program more quickly and efficiently. Some tips may help you use the C programming environment more effectively. Others may provide handy programming ideas to help you write well-constructed programs.

Detailed descriptions of how a program works are indicated by this icon. This type of box appears after nearly every program listing and supplements the explanation given in the text.

IN SIMPLE TERMS

In a few instances in this book, some VERY important information is tagged with this icon. Be sure to read any paragraphs flagged with this little picture.

CATCH THIS!

Step into the Strange and Wonderful World of C

Still with us? Good news! Just around the corner is your first C programming lesson. We could stay here and chat all day, or you could turn the page and start on your fun-filled vacation in C-land. See you there.

CHAPTER 1

A Programming Primer

(Stepping into the Dark Unknown)

IN A NUTSHELL

▼ Knowing reasons to program

▼ Discovering what comprises a program

▼ Learning about different computer languages

▼ Writing a computer program

C FOR ROOKIES

Before you get started with computer programming, it might help to have a basic understanding of what it's all about. You undoubtedly have some ideas about what a program is and how it works, or you wouldn't have bought this book to begin with. Some of these ideas may be right on the money; others may be as crazy as a whale in a tutu.

Whatever your ideas about programming, this chapter gives you the skinny, the real poop, the absolute truth. After reading this chapter, you may find that your perceptions about programming are pretty solid; or you may find that you know as much about programming a computer as you do about building a submarine. In either case, you'll be a better person for having spent time here. If nothing else, you're about to learn a surprising secret—and everyone likes secrets.

The Surprising Secret

(Mum's the word)

The computer programming world has a well-kept secret. You won't hear programmers talking about it (which is, of course, why it's a secret). And if you've been using a computer for any length of time, you'll probably find this secret hard to believe. Nevertheless, it's as true as the sky is blue. So brace yourself. You're about to learn a shocking fact. Ready?

Computers are stupid.

It's true! Just how stupid are they? Computers are so stupid, they make avocados look like brain surgeons. Fact is, a computer can do absolutely nothing on its own. Without programmers, computers are as useless as rubber razors. Computers can do only what they're told to do. And if you think for a minute, you'll realize this means computers can only perform tasks that humans already know how to do. So why do we bother with computers? The great thing about computers is not that they're smart,

but that they can perform endless calculations quickly and without getting bored and turning on reruns of "The Love Boat."

Programmers are the people who tell computers what to do. That's not to say that when you use your computer you're programming it. For example, when you plop yourself down in front of a word processor and hack out a letter to Aunt Martha, you're not giving commands to the computer. You're only using the commands contained in the program. It's the computer program—which was written by a programmer—that actually tells the computer what to do.

Fig. 1 shows the relationship between a computer user, a program, and a computer. That's you, the computer user, way up at the top of the hierarchy. (Feeling dizzy?) You probably use your computer for many activities besides word processing, such as organizing data in a spreadsheet, keeping track of information in a database, and maybe even playing games. In all these cases, you write a program, which provides instructions to the computer.

Fig. 1

The bottom line is that if you want to give commands directly to your computer, you must learn to write programs. But, then, that's why you bought this book.

C FOR ROOKIES

Why Learn to Program?

(What's in it for me?)

Most people need a reason to do the things they do. For instance, consider the case of Ed Beagley, a sanitary engineer (all right, a garbage collector) from River Falls, Vermont. Ed gets up in the morning because he doesn't want to be late for work. Ed eats a good breakfast so he doesn't get hungry before lunch. Ed does his job well so he can collect a paycheck at the end of the week. Finally, Ed takes a bath at the end of the day because, well, he does deal with a lot of garbage.

Just as Ed has reasons for the way he lives his life, you probably have some reasons to learn computer programming. And there are as many reasons for learning to program as there are raisins in California. Only you know what it is about computer programming that makes you want to learn it, but some common reasons are:

▼ You're looking for a fun and rewarding hobby.

▼ You want to be able to write the programs you really need—the ones you can't always find at the software store.

▼ You want to learn more about how computers work.

▼ You have to learn programming for school or work.

▼ You want to impress your friends.

▼ Some misguided person gave you this book as a gift, and you don't want to hurt his or her feelings.

These all are legitimate reasons. You may have a better one, but whatever your reason, once you get started with programming, you'll find that it can be both fascinating and addictive. Your spouse or significant other, however, may ban computers from your home and burn this book

after he or she realizes just how addictive computer programming can be. Consider yourself warned.

What's a Computer Program?

(Looks like Greek to me)

Did you ever build a model airplane? When you opened the box, you found a list of numbered instructions. By following the instructions in the order in which they were presented, you put your model together piece by piece. When you finally reached the last instruction, your model was complete—except, of course, for those few parts that are always left over.

A computer program is much like that list of instructions, except the instructions in a computer program don't tell *you* what to do. They tell the computer what to do.

Still, a computer program is nothing more than a list of commands. The computer follows these commands, one by one, until it reaches the end of the program. Unlike when you built your model, however, the computer will have no left-over pieces. Computers are stupid, not sloppy.

PLAY BALL!

BUZZWORD

Computer Program

A computer program is a list of instructions the computer follows from beginning to end. A computer programmer writes this list of instructions using one of the many computer languages.

Each line in a computer program is usually a single command that the computer must obey. Each command does only a very small task, such as printing a name on-screen or adding two numbers. When you put

C FOR ROOKIES

hundreds, thousands, or even hundreds of thousands of these commands together, your computer can do wonderful things: balance a checkbook, print a document, draw pictures, or blast invading aliens from the sky.

As you see in the next section, computer programs can be written in one of many different languages.

Programming Languages

(Parlez-Vous C?)

Computers don't understand English. They're stupid, remember? They can't, in fact, even understand the C programming language. They're *really* stupid. Computers understand only one thing, machine language, which is entirely composed of numbers. Unfortunately, many human minds don't deal well with numbers. Imagine, for example, a human language in which the numbers 10, 12, 14, and 15 have the following significance:

10 hello

12 you

14 how

15 are

BUZZWORD

Machine Language

Machine language is a list of numbers that act as instructions to the computer. It is the lowest level at which a computer is programmed. That is, machine language is the level of instructions that the computer operates at.

Now, imagine walking up to a friend and saying "10 14 15 12?" Your friend wouldn't know what to say. (If your friend answers "32 65 34," he spends way too much time with computers. Get him help.) Nope, if you expect your friend to respond, you'd better use the words "Hello, how are you?" Conversely, if we mere mortals have any hope of making sense of machine language, we have to change it into something we can understand, something that has as little to do with numbers as a vegetarian has to do with steak. That's where C (or any other computer language) comes in.

Now, wait a minute. Computers understand only numbers, right? C programs use words and symbols (and a few numbers) so people can understand the program. How, then, can the computer understand and run the program? The truth is, before you can run a C program you must *compile* it.

PLAY BALL!

BUZZWORD

Compiler

A *compiler* changes your program into an *executable file* that can be run from the DOS prompt. Some languages are compiler-based, some are not. Almost all implementations of the C programming language use a compiler.

There are all kinds of computer languages, including Pascal, C, C++, FORTRAN, COBOL, Modula-2, and BASIC. All computer languages have one thing in common: they can be read by humans.

Some languages, such as BASIC, convert a program to machine language one line at a time as the program runs. Other languages, such as C and Pascal, use a compiler to convert the entire program before any of the program runs. All programming languages must be converted to machine language in order for the computer to understand the program.

Interpreter

An *interpreter* is a program that changes programs into machine language that the computer can understand. An interpreter, like Microsoft's QBasic, translates a program as it is executing. This is different from a compiler, which translates the code before executing the program.

The Programming Process

(Getting down to the nitty-gritty)

Now that you know something about computer programs, how do you go about creating one? Writing a computer program, though not particularly difficult, can be a long and tedious process. It's much like writing a term paper for school or a financial report for your boss. You start out with a basic idea of what you want to do and write a first draft. After reading over the draft and resisting the urge to throw the pages into the fireplace, you go back to polishing your prose until it glows like a gem in the sun. Over the course of the writing process, you may write many drafts before you're satisfied with the document you've produced.

Writing a program requires development steps similar to those you use when writing a paper or report. The following list outlines these steps:

1. Type the program using C's editor.

2. Save the program to disk.

3. Compile the program with the C compiler.

4. Run the program and see how it works.

5. Fix programming errors.

6. Go back to Step 2.

As you can see, most of the steps in the programming process are repeated over and over again as errors are discovered and corrected. Even experienced programmers seldom write programs that are error-free. Programmers spend more time fine-tuning their programs than they do writing them initially, which is why they eat so many Gummy Bears and drink so much Coke. All that rewriting saps their energy and lowers their blood-sugar levels.

This fine-tuning is important because we humans are not as logical as we like to think. Moreover, our minds are incapable of remembering every detail required to make a program run perfectly. Heck, most of us are lucky if we can remember our telephone numbers. Only when a program crashes or does something else unexpected can we hope to find those sneaky errors that hide in programs. Computer experts say that there's no such thing as a bug-free program. After you start writing full-length programs, you'll see how true this statement is.

PLAY BALL!

BUZZWORD

Bugs

Bugs are programming errors that stop your program from running correctly. Bugs are also nasty creatures with spindly legs and crunchy shells that make you scream when they leap out of shadows. But this book doesn't deal with that type of bug, so we won't mention them here.

Is Programming Easy?

(Squashing that panic attack)

After reading all that's involved in writing and running a computer program, you might be a little nervous. After all, you bought this book because it promised to teach you computer programming. No one warned you about such mysterious topics as machine language, interpreters, compilers, and program bugs. So, is programming easy or not?

Well, yes and no.

It's easy to learn to write simple programs with C. The C language is logical. With only minimal practice, you can write many useful and fun programs with C. All you need is the time to read this book and the ambition to write a few programs of your own. In fact, what you'll learn in this book is enough programming for just about anyone who's not planning to be a professional programmer.

However, if you want to make programming a career, you have much to learn that's not covered in this introductory book. For example, consider a word processing program like WordPerfect, which took dozens of programmers many years to write. To write such complex software, you must have intimate knowledge of how your computer works; you must have spent many years learning the intricacies of professional computer programming.

Still, there's a lot you can do with C, whether you're interested in writing utilities, simple applications, or even games. And, once you get the hang of it, you'll discover that programming in C is not as difficult as you may have thought.

After all, computers may be stupid, but you're not.

Summing Up

▼ A computer can do only what a human instructs it to do.

▼ There are many reasons to learn to program, but if nothing else, programming is a rewarding hobby.

▼ A computer program is a list of commands that the computer follows from beginning to end.

▼ There are many computer languages. The language you learn in this book is called C.

▼ A C program must be converted to machine language before the computer can understand it. This conversion is done by a C compiler.

▼ Writing a program is a lot like writing a text document. You must write several "drafts" before the program is complete.

▼ Programming with C is as easy or difficult as you want it to be.

In the next chapter, we will take a look at how to use the Personal C compiler and Turbo Edit, two programming tools included with this book. You will learn how to write a simple program, and how to use the compiler to convert that program into a form that the computer can understand. So, grab your riding gloves, and let's get ready to start the journey.

CHAPTER 2
Welcome to C
(Let the Fun Begin)

IN A NUTSHELL

▼ Running C

▼ Giving commands to C

▼ Loading, saving, and printing programs

▼ Typing program text

▼ Editing program text

▼ Finding words or phrases in a program

Now that you have a general idea of what a computer program is and how it works, it's time to load up a C compiler and get to work.

Many different C compilers are available. The most popular are from Borland and Microsoft. Borland sells Turbo C++ and Borland C++ (these are actually two different products). Microsoft sells C/C++ 7 with Programmers Workbench, and Visual C++.

"Wait a minute," you might be thinking. "This book is supposed to be about C, not C++. What's going on here?" The answer is that both of the aforementioned C++ compilers also have built-in C compilers. This turns out to be the deal of the century. Not only do you get a C compiler, you also get a C++ compiler. You can read about C++ in the sequel to this book, C++ *for Veterans* (just kidding).

However, you don't have to worry about purchasing a C compiler. If you have one, great. But as the proud purchaser of this book, you are provided with a C compiler called Personal C Compiler (PCC) on the diskette included with this book. You also get a text editor, which enables you to type your C programs. This editor is called Turbo Edit.

In this chapter, you learn about the Personal C Compiler and Turbo Edit. You'll use these tools to write your first C program. If you've used a word processor before, this chapter covers a lot of familiar ground. If you have no experience with text editing, you should carefully study the discussions that follow. After all, you can't write a program until you know how to type it!

Diving into DOS

(What you need to know)

As you might already know, your computer's operating system is called MS-DOS, which stands for *most skunks don oval slippers*. (If you believe

that, close this book now; you have no hope of becoming a programmer.) Actually, MS-DOS stands for Microsoft Disk Operating System. This operating system, just like any other program, is software installed on your computer. It might have already been installed when you bought your computer, or you might have installed it yourself. In either case, there should be a directory on your hard disk named DOS, which is where MS-DOS hides.

BUZZWORD

MS-DOS

Your computer's operating system is named MS-DOS—Microsoft Disk Operating System. Called DOS for short, this operating system is loaded into your computer's memory when you turn on the computer. Without DOS loaded, your computer does nothing but sit uselessly on your desk.

If you look in the DOS directory, you'll find almost 100 or more files. Most of these files make up the MS-DOS operating system and DOS commands. To learn to program, you must memorize all the filenames in the DOS directory and be prepared to recite them in alphabetical order. (Just kidding.) However, you should have some idea of which DOS commands are useful and which are used most often.

Installing the Book Disk

(Getting up and running)

Before you can use the Personal C Compiler, you must install it. Installation is the process of putting the Personal C Compiler program files on your computer's hard disk drive. This installation process actually does a little bit more than that, but the important thing to remember is that it copies the compiler to a directory on your hard disk drive.

Before installing the Personal C Compiler, you need to check the amount of free space available on your hard drive. The Personal C Compiler requires at least 1 megabyte of hard disk space.

To begin the installation process, put the disk in your floppy drive and type *n:*, where *n* is the floppy drive that contains the installation disk (usually A or B). Next, type **INSTALL** *n*, in which *n* is the hard drive where you want the compiler files installed (usually C or D).

The installation routine copies the files to your hard disk in a directory named CROOK. That's all there is to installing the Personal C Compiler. That wasn't too bad, was it? And the good news is that this installation process has to be done only once.

Loading Turbo Edit

(Every journey starts with the first step)

Before you can compile a C program or write programs of your own, you must load Turbo Edit. This is no different from having to load a word processor before writing a document—except with Turbo Edit, you'll never feel obligated to write a letter to weird Uncle Henry. Turbo Edit is actually very similar to a word processing program, except you use it to write programs. To load Turbo Edit, switch to the CROOK directory, type **TVEDIT**, and press Enter. When you do, you see the screen shown in Fig. 1.

Turbo Edit's main screen is made up of several smaller elements:

Menu Bar: You access Turbo Edit's various commands through this menu.

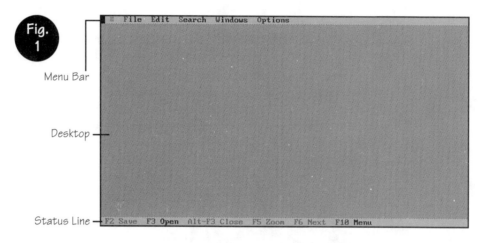

Fig. 1

Menu Bar

Desktop

Status Line

```
≡  File  Edit  Search  Windows  Options
```

```
F2 Save  F3 Open  Alt-F3 Close  F5 Zoom  F6 Next  F10 Menu
```

Desktop: The desktop is the background gray pattern on which all windows are displayed. It provides an area for you to work with multiple windows and move them around the screen.

Status Line: The status line shows the keys you can press to access certain commands. The status line also provides a quick description of any highlighted menu command.

Now that you know how the Turbo Edit main screen is set up, let's take a closer look at this powerful editing environment.

Using Turbo Edit's Menu Bar

(A look at today's specials)

Computers are stupid, and so is Turbo Edit. You can sit at your desk and stare at Turbo Edit's main screen as long as you like, but until you give it a command, it'll just sit there staring back. And you'll always be the first to blink.

As in many computer programs, you can use your keyboard or your mouse to give commands to Turbo Edit. To select commands with your keyboard, tap the F10 key to activate the menu bar at the top of the screen. A green box appears around the **File** menu title. A highlighted box shows which menu will open when you press Enter.

To select the menu you want, use your keyboard's left-and right-arrow keys to move the green box. When the box is on the menu you want, press Enter to open the menu.

TIP

You can open any menu instantly by holding down the Alt key while pressing the first letter of the menu's title. For example, to open the **File** menu, press Alt-F. The letter F is called a shortcut key. The shortcut key will always be the same letter as the first letter of the menu choice, but it is not always the first letter of the menu option.

When the menu appears, use your keyboard's up- and down-arrow keys to highlight the command you want. Press Enter to issue the highlighted command.

Using a mouse to select menu commands is a little easier. Place the mouse pointer over the menu title and click the left mouse button. When the menu drops down, use the mouse to click the command you want to issue.

Don't fret about what all the menu commands do. You'll learn about them later. But for now, how about using the **File** menu to have a little fun?

Loading a C Program

(Lights, camera, action!)

Before you can run a C program, the program must be loaded and compiled. This doesn't mean that you should force your program to chug-a-lug a quart of Smirnoff's. Rather, it means that you must bring the program's text file (called the *source code*) into Turbo Edit's editor window. You do this with the **O**pen… command of the **F**ile menu, which is shown in Fig. 2. When you select the **O**pen command, you see the Open File dialog box shown in Fig. 3.

TIP

Every time you see a command that ends with three dots (called an *ellipsis*), the command will activate a dialog box. The dialog box usually enables you to enter additional information to carry out a command.

Fig.
2

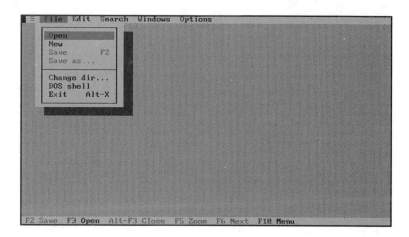

C FOR ROOKIES

Fig. 3

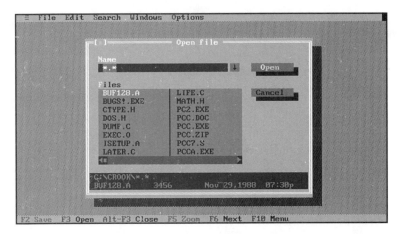

```
≡ File Edit Search Windows Options

══[■]═════════════════════ Open file ═══════════════════════
  Name
  *.*                                    ↓    ┌──────────┐
                                              │   Open   │
  Files                                       └──────────┘
  BUF128.A        LIFE.C
  BUGS!.EXE       MATH.H                       ┌──────────┐
  CTYPE.H         PC2.EXE                       │  Cancel  │
  DOS.H           PCC.DOC                       └──────────┘
  DUMP.C          PCC.EXE
  EXEC.O          PCC.ZIP
  ISETUP.A        PCC7.S
  LATER.C         PCCA.EXE
  ◄■                                     ►

 C:\CROOK\*.*
  BUF128.A      3456          Nov 29,1988  07:30p

F2 Save  F3 Open  Alt-F3 Close  F5 Zoom  F6 Next  F10 Menu
```

PLAY BALL!

BUZZWORD

Source Code

Source code is the program text that you type into an editor. With compiled languages (such as C), a program's source code is no longer needed after the program is compiled. Still, programmers usually save their source code so that they can make changes or additions to the program. Programmers also save their source code so that they can impress friends and attract members of the opposite sex with their cleverness.

Like menus, dialog boxes enable you to make selections with either your keyboard or your mouse. To load a file using the keyboard, type the name of the file you want to load, and press Enter. Or, if you want to avoid typing the filename, press Tab to move the cursor to the **Files** list box. Use the up- and down-arrow keys to highlight the file you want, and press Enter to load the files.

PLAY BALL!

BUZZWORD

Tabbing

The process of moving around a dialog box is called *tabbing*. By repeatedly pressing the Tab key, you move the cursor from field to field inside the dialog box. A dialog box can have several different types of fields. Besides fields that allow you to type text, there are also fields such as *buttons* and *list boxes*. Buttons are fields that you tab to and then select by pressing Enter. List boxes don't enable you to type any new text; instead, they enable you to choose an item from a list of items.

You can select any button at the right side of the dialog box by repeatedly pressing the Tab key. Press Enter when the desired button is highlighted.

There are two methods of selecting a file using your mouse: double-click the desired filename in the Files list box, or click on the filename once to highlight it, then click the Open button at the bottom of the dialog box.

If you change your mind about opening a file, just select the Cancel button.

Try opening the sample program named LIFE.C, which is located in the CROOK subdirectory on the drive that you installed the book disk on (the default drive is C:). After opening this file, your screen should look like Fig. 4. If your screen doesn't look like this figure, you've either opened the wrong file or you're overdue for an eye examination.

LIFE.C is a classic program, originally written by John Conway, which demonstrates a sample population of people as it changes over many generations.

C FOR ROOKIES

Fig.
4

```
 ≡  File  Edit  Search  Windows  Options
┌─[■]════════════════════ C:\CROOK\LIFE.C ═══════════════════[↕]─┐
│ /*      LIFE.C          The much implemented game of Life invented by John Con│
│                                                                               │
│                              This version was written to illustrate the use   │
│                              screen and keyboard interface. Use C option fo    │
│                                                                               │
│                              To generate:                                     │
│                              C LIFE                              */            │
│                                                                               │
│                                                                               │
│                                                                               │
│ /*                                                                            │
│   global constant and data declarations                                      │
│ */                                                                            │
│                                                                               │
│ #define ROWS     24                                                           │
│ #define COLS     80                                                           │
│                                                                               │
│ /* control key translations */                                               │
│ #define up_char 30                                                            │
│ #define down_char      31                                                     │
│ #define left_char 29                                                          │
└─ 1:1 ═══◄■───────────────────────────────────────────────────────────────┘
 F2 Save  F3 Open  Alt-F3 Close  F5 Zoom  F6 Next  F10 Menu
```

Go ahead and give LIFE.C a shot. To compile and run the program, exit Turbo Edit by pressing Alt-X. From the DOS ready prompt, type **C LIFE**. The compiler is loaded, and your program is compiled and linked (see Fig. 5). Any error messages that occur (none should) are displayed on-screen. When the linker is done, you return to the DOS prompt.

Fig.
5

```
c:\crook>C LIFE
pcc LIFE
PCC Compiler     V1.2d Copyright by Mark DeSmet, 1993
end of PCC       06D4 code   0A2A data      9% utilizationpccl LIFE pcio
PCCL Linker for PCC V1.2d - Copyright Mark DeSmet, 1993
end of PCCL      10% utilization
c:\crook>
```

Fig. 6 shows a general edit/compile/link cycle.

C FOR ROOKIES

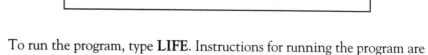

Fig.
6

To run the program, type **LIFE**. Instructions for running the program are displayed (see Fig. 7).

Fig.
7

```
                The game of Life by John Conway

                   Use LIFE C with color monitor.
            If started with a number, a random pattern starts the game.

        Otherwise, move the cursor with the four arrow keys to create life.

            DEL changes cursor movement to mean that cells are deleted

                     INS flips back to create mode.

            The '+' key will toggle the game on or off.

                        Hit ESC to bail out.

            Enter starting number of cells or hit CR
```

The simulation works like this: After you press Enter to clear the instruction screen, you first use the arrow keys to generate an artificial population of people (small faces). When you are ready to see how that population reacts, press the + key to start the simulation (see Fig. 8). You will probably want to experiment with several different beginning population settings.

After you have experimented with the LIFE.C program, return to Turbo Edit by typing **TVEDIT LIFE.C** from the DOS prompt. This time, Turbo Edit automatically loads the source file from disk. This is a shortcut, so you don't have to bring up the Open File dialog box as you did earlier.

Fig. 8

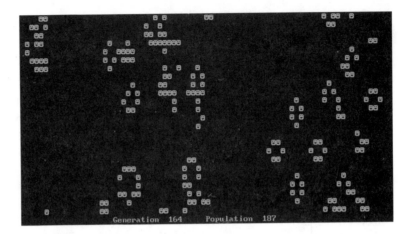

Generation 164   Population 187

Controlling the Edit Window

(Arrows and scrollers and cursors, oh my!)

By now you've probably noticed that Turbo Edit's editor window has a couple of extra controls. Along the right side and bottom are scroll bars that enable you to view parts of the program that are off-screen. You can scroll the program in the edit window up or down a line by clicking the scroll bar's up or down arrows with your mouse. Likewise, you can scroll left or right a character at a time by clicking the horizontal scroll bar's arrows.

To scroll up or down a full page, click anywhere inside the vertical scroll bar above or below the scroll thumb, respectively. Scrolling horizontally works the same way, except you click inside the horizontal scroll bar. The scroll thumb is the white box that appears in the scroll bar. You can move instantly to any place in a program by placing your mouse cursor over a scroll thumb, holding down the left mouse button, and moving the scroll thumb to the approximate location you want.

To scroll a program using the keyboard, use the arrow keys or the Page Up and Page Down keys.

C FOR ROOKIES

Typing Programs

(The pitter-patter of little keys)

Running a program that comes with the Personal C Compiler is fun, but that's not why you're reading this book. You're reading this book because you want to learn to program—or because somebody has your copy of *People*. In any case, to write programs, you must learn to use Turbo Edit. In this section, you learn to do just that.

To start a new program, you need an empty edit window. To open one, select the **N**ew option from the **F**ile menu. A new window named *Untitled* is opened. You'll type the commands that make up your C program into this window. Before typing a new program, however, you should give the empty window an appropriate name. (Names like *Adrian*, *Samantha*, and *Guido the Man* are out.) To name your program, first select the **S**ave As… entry of the **F**ile menu. You then see the dialog box shown in Fig. 9.

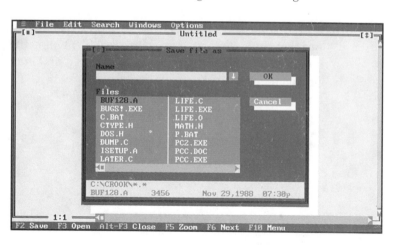

When the Name edit box appears, type the filename **TEST.C** into the Save File As edit box. When you're finished, press Enter or click the dialog's **OK** button with your mouse. The name of the window changes to TEST.C.

C FOR ROOKIES

NOTE

All your C programs should use the file extension .C because that's the extension C compilers expect C programs to have. Moreover, that's the extension that other programmers use. The .CPP extension that you will come across in compilers from Borland and Microsoft is the extension for C++ programs.

Now that you have a newly named program window, you can type your program. Try typing the program in Listing 2.1 into the editor window. Make sure you type the program exactly as it is listed here. You must use upper- and lowercase letters *exactly as they are listed*, because unlike other languages, the C programming language is *case-sensitive*. That means it notices the difference between uppercase and lowercase characters. Therefore, if you do not type words correctly, the compiler won't recognize them. Remember, the compiler is stupid.

With that piece of advice, go ahead and type the program in Listing 2.1 into the editor window. If you don't feel like typing the program, go ahead and load the file PROG1.C, which is found in the C:\CROOK subdirectory installed on your hard drive by the INSTALL batch file. Then take a quick glance through the program listing.

Listing 2.1. Your first C program

```
#include <stdio.h>

int main()
{
   char name[255];
   int x;

   printf("What is your name? ");
   scanf("%s", &name);

   for (x=1; x<=200; x++)
```

```
   printf("%s", name);

   return 0;
}
```

PLAY BALL!

BUZZWORD

	Keyword

A *keyword* is a word that is part of a programming language. Keywords, also known as *reserved words*, cannot be used for anything else in a program.

There are several parts to the above program. The first statement, which looks like this,

```
#include <stdio.h>
```

tells the compiler to include information about certain keywords that are going to be used in the program. Although these two statements are very cryptic, don't worry—you don't need to know what they do and how they work just yet. All you need to know at this point is that this information comes as part of the Personal C Compiler package.

The next section of the program is the declaration section. The declarations of the program tell the compiler where to start executing the program and what memory will be used. It looks like this:

```
int main()
{
   char name[255];
   int x;
```

The `main()` statement just tells the C compiler the main entry point for the program. This is where program execution is to begin. The funny-looking symbol on the next line is called the *brace*. You will see a lot of braces in this book. The brace marks the beginning of a section of instructions.

C FOR ROOKIES

The `char name[255]` statement declares a space in memory for character data. The number 255 refers to how many characters can be stored. The `int x` statement declares a place in memory that stores an integer value.

The program now displays a message to the user, and then receives information from the user. The following lines carry it out:

```
printf("What is your name? ");
scanf("%s", &name);
```

You'll see a lot of lines starting with `printf`—that's a statement you as a programmer use to communicate with the program's user. In short, `printf` displays information on-screen. In this case, we're asking the user for his or her name.

Another statement you will see much of is the `scanf` statement. It lets the user enter information, which is then stored within your program. The data that is entered (in this case, the person's name) is stored in the area previously declared as `name`.

Finally, the rest of the program displays the user's name 200 times—not terribly useful, but it illustrates a cool feature of virtually all programming languages (which you'll learn about in Chapter 8, "Powerful Structures"). The instructions look like this:

```
for (x=1; x<=200; x++)
    printf("%s", name);

return 0;
}
```

The return statement returns a value to DOS. This value can be used in DOS batch files to check for a return value from a program. The ANSI C specification calls for every program to return a value. Because of this, a value is returned; however, because the value won't be used, we return a value of zero.

C FOR ROOKIES

That last funny-looking symbol is a closing brace. It works with the opening brace that appears at the beginning of the program. These braces actually act in pairs. As mentioned earlier, they mark sections of code that belong together.

Your screen should now look like Fig. 10. If you don't see the entire contents of the editor window, you can press the F5 key to enlarge the editor window to the maximum size possible.

Fig. 10

```
  File   Edit   Search   Windows   Options
[■]                     C:\CROOK\PROG1.C                        [↕]
#include <stdio.h>

int main()
{
   char name[255];
   int x;

   printf("What is your name? ");
   scanf("%s", &name);

   for (x=1; x<=200; x++)
      printf("%s", name);

   return 0;
}

     1:1      ◄■
F2 Save   F3 Open   Alt-F3 Close   F5 Zoom   F6 Next   F10 Menu
```

Soon you will compile and run the program and see what it does. But first, you should save your program to disk so that you won't lose your work if anything goes wrong when you run it. It's possible for a programming error to lock up your computer, forcing you to restart the computer. It's also possible for a programming error to infuriate you enough to throw your computer out the nearest window. In either case, you'll be glad you saved your program first.

To save your program, select the Save entry of the File menu. After selecting this command, your program is safely stored on your disk under the name PROG1.C (or whatever you named the program).

To compile the program, exit Turbo Edit by pressing Alt-X. Now type
C PROG1 at the DOS prompt. This compiles and links the program.

The program first asks you to enter your name. Type your name and
press Enter. You should then see something similar to the text below
flash on-screen, and you will be returned to the DOS prompt:

```
c:\crook>prog1
What is your name? John
JohnJohnJohnJohnJohnJohnJohnJohnJohnJohnJohnJohnJohnJohnJohnJohnJohnJohnJohn
JohnJohnJohnJohnJohnJohnJohnJohnJohnJohnJohnJohnJohnJohnJohnJohnJohnJohnJohn
JohnJohnJohnJohnJohnJohnJohnJohnJohnJohnJohnJohnJohnJohnJohnJohnJohnJohnJohn
JohnJohnJohnJohnJohnJohnJohnJohnJohnJohnJohnJohnJohnJohnJohnJohnJohnJohnJohn
JohnJohnJohnJohnJohnJohnJohnJohnJohnJohnJohnJohnJohnJohnJohnJohnJohnJohnJohn
JohnJohnJohnJohnJohnJohnJohnJohnJohnJohnJohnJohnJohnJohnJohnJohnJohnJohnJohn
JohnJohnJohnJohnJohnJohnJohnJohnJohnJohnJohnJohnJohnJohnJohnJohnJohnJohnJohn
JohnJohnJohnJohnJohnJohnJohnJohnJohnJohnJohnJohnJohnJohnJohnJohnJohnJohnJohn
JohnJohnJohnJohnJohnJohnJohnJohnJohnJohnJohnJohnJohnJohnJohnJohnJohnJohnJohn
JohnJohnJohnJohnJohnJohnJohnJohnJohnJohnJohnJohnJohnJohnJohnJohnJohnJohnJohn

c:\crook>
```

Congratulations! You've just written and run your first C program. Pat
yourself on the back, go get a snack, and brag until everyone in your
household is thoroughly annoyed.

Don't worry if you don't understand even one single line of this first
program. The purpose here is just to get you familiar with the Personal C
Compiler. We'll cover every statement in this first program in detail
over the course of the next few chapters.

Printing a Program

(A masterpiece suitable for framing)

If you have a printer connected to your system, you can print copies of
your programs. You don't have to print your programs, but you might

want to have copies on paper that you can store in a file. Also, it's often easier to find programming errors by looking at a printout of a program than by looking at the program on-screen. More importantly, printing programs uses up ink and paper, which makes it look like you're actually accomplishing something. (Of course, using paper also kills trees, so you might want to examine your priorities.)

How about printing the program you just wrote? To do this, make sure you are at the DOS prompt and type **P PROG1.C**. The program listing will be output to your printer. This batch file assumes you have a parallel printer. If you have a serial printer, you will want to follow the directions that come with your printer.

Cutting, Copying, and Pasting

(Kindergarten for programmers)

Every text editor worthy of the name enables you to select text blocks and manipulate them in various ways. Turbo Edit also enables you to perform these handy functions. You can find the text-editing functions in the Edit menu, which is shown in Fig. 11.

NOTE

You can access edit functions directly from the keyboard, without bothering with the Edit menu, by pressing the shortcut keys shown in the Edit menu. For example, to Cut a block of text, press Shift-Del. To Paste the cut text back into your program, press Shift-Ins. After you learn these hot keys, you can select editing functions quickly and conveniently.

C FOR ROOKIES

Fig.
11

```
≡  File  Edit  Search  Windows  Options
┌─[■]─────────────────────── C:\CROOK\PROG1.C ──────────────────[↕]─┐
│          ┌──────────────────┐                                     │
│#include  │                  │                                     │
│          │ Cut     Shift-Del│                                     │
│int main  │ Copy    Ctrl-Ins │                                     │
│{         │ Paste   Shift-Ins│                                     │
│   char   │ Show clipboard   │                                     │
│   int x  │                  │                                     │
│          │ Clear   Ctrl-Del │                                     │
│   print  └──────────────────┘");                                  │
│   scanf("%s", &name);                                             │
│   scr_clr();                                                      │
│                                                                   │
│   for (x=1; x<=200; x++)                                          │
│      printf("%s", name);                                          │
│                                                                   │
│   return 0;                                                       │
│}                                                                  │
│                                                                   │
│──── 1:1 ──◄■                                                      │
└───────────────────────────────────────────────────────────────────┘
 F2 Save  F3 Open  Alt-F3 Close  F5 Zoom  F6 Next  F10 Menu
```

PLAY BALL!

BUZZWORD

Hot Key

You don't have to worry about burning your fingertips by touching a *hot key*. A hot key is a keystroke that instantly selects a menu command without you having to access the menu. This is an especially fast way to perform tasks such as text editing. Unfortunately, although hot keys are convenient, not all menu commands have them.

Start Turbo Edit by typing **TVEDIT** and pressing Enter. Before you can use editing functions, you must select the text those functions will manipulate. Fig. 12 shows what a selected block of text looks like. You can select text using either your keyboard or your mouse.

To select text from the keyboard, use the arrow keys to position the blinking text cursor anywhere on the first line of the text block. Then, hold down the Shift key and press the down-arrow key to highlight the lines in the block. Each time you press the down arrow, you highlight another line of text.

To select text with the mouse, place the mouse pointer on the first line you want to select, hold down the left mouse button, and drag the mouse pointer down to the last line in the block.

Fig. 12

```
 ≡  File  Edit  Search  Windows  Options
┌─[■]─────────────────── C:\CROOK\PROG1.C ════════════════[↕]═┐
│                                                             │
│#include <stdio.h>                                           │
│                                                             │
│int main()                                                   │
│{                                                            │
│   char name[255];                                           │
│   int x;                                                    │
│                                                             │
│   printf("What is your name? ");                            │
│   scanf("%s", &name);                                       │
│                                                             │
│   for (x=1; x<=200; x++)                                     │
│      printf("%s", name);                                    │
│                                                             │
│   return 0;                                                 │
│}                                                            │
│                                                             │
│──── 12:1 ───◀■─────────────────────────────────────►        │
F2 Save  F3 Open  Alt-F3 Close  F5 Zoom  F6 Next  F10 Menu
```

Try selecting some text now. Using either the keyboard or mouse technique, select the middle three lines of your program's text, as shown in Fig. 12.

After you select the text, open the Edit menu. The Cut, Copy, and Clear menu commands are now enabled. The Cut command removes the highlighted text from the screen and places it into Turbo Edit's *clipboard*—a special text buffer from which you can later paste the text back into your program, perhaps in a different location. The Copy command also places the selected text into the clipboard, but it does so without removing the text from the screen. Finally, the Clear command removes the selected text from the screen, but does not place it into the clipboard.

CAUTION

When you select the Clear entry of the Edit menu, any text you have highlighted is deleted forever, so use this command with care.

For now, select the Copy command. When you do, the **E**dit menu closes; you're back at Turbo Edit's editor window. Everything looks the same, but now a copy of the highlighted text is in Turbo Edit's clipboard.

To use the clipboard, first unhighlight the selected text block by pressing any arrow key on your keyboard or by clicking your left mouse button. (Actually, you should click your *mouse's* left mouse button. If *you* have a left mouse button, consult a surgeon immediately.) Look at the **E**dit menu again. Because there is no longer a text block selected, the Cut, Copy, and Clear entries are no longer highlighted. However, the **P**aste entry is highlighted. This tells you that there is text in the clipboard. In this case, it's the text you just copied.

Start Turbo Edit by typing **TVEDIT** and pressing Enter. Close the **E**dit menu, place the blinking text cursor on the first blank line below your program, and select the **P**aste command. The text you copied is pasted into your program at the text cursor's location.

TIP

If you select the **P**aste command while a text block is highlighted on-screen, the text in the clipboard replaces the highlighted text. Similarly, if you start typing when you have a text block highlighted, whatever you type replaces the highlighted text.

Searching and Replacing

(The lost-and-found department)

In a small program, such as the one you just wrote, it's easy to find specific words or phrases. For example, if you want to find the keyword printf, just glance at the screen, and there it is. In large programs,

however, finding text visually is tougher than chasing an angry bear up a tree. Luckily, Turbo Edit includes search commands. These commands are, of course, found in the Search menu, which is shown in Fig. 13.

```
 ≡  File  Edit  Search  Windows  Options
 [■]                              :\CROOK\PROG1.C                          [↕]
                    Find...
#include <stdi    Replace...
                  Search again
int main()
{
    char name[255];
    int x;

    printf("What is your name? ");
    scanf("%s", &name);
    scr_clr();

    for (x=1; x<=200; x++)
        printf("%s", name);

    return 0;
}
     1:1
 F2 Save  F3 Open  Alt-F3 Close  F5 Zoom  F6 Next  F10 Menu
```

As you can see, the Search menu contains several entries, the first three being **Find...**, **Replace...**, and **Search again**. To find the next occurrence (starting at the text cursor's location) of any word or phrase, select the **Find...** entry from the Search menu. You'll see the dialog box shown in Fig. 14.

```
 ≡  File  Edit  Search  Windows  Options
 [■]                         C:\CROOK\PROG1.C                          [↕]
#include <stdio.h>

int main()
{                    [ ]              Find
    char name[255];
    int x;          Text to find
                    ┌─────────────────────────────┐ ↓
    printf("What is y
    scanf("%s", &name   [ ] Case sensitive
    scr_clr();          [ ] Whole words only

    for (x=1; x<=200;
        printf("%s", n          OK            Cancel

    return 0;
}

     1:1
 F2 Save  F3 Open  Alt-F3 Close  F5 Zoom  F6 Next  F10 Menu
```

When the Find dialog box appears, the word at the text cursor's location appears in the Text to find edit box. If this is the word you want to search for, press Enter to start the search. If you want to look for a different word or phrase, just type it into the Text to find edit box and press Enter. If you don't want to search for a word or phrase, you might want to ask yourself why the heck you're staring at the Find dialog box.

Try the **Find**… command now, by following these steps:

1. Press Ctrl-Page Up to place the blinking text cursor at the beginning of your program.

2. Select the **Find**… entry of the Search menu. The Find dialog box appears.

3. In the Text to find edit box, type the word **name** and press Enter. Turbo Edit finds and highlights the first occurrence of the word *name*.

4. Select OK to begin the search.

5. To find other occurrences of this word, select the Search again entry of the Search menu, or just press Ctrl-L. Each time you select this command, Turbo Edit finds another occurrence of the word *name*.

Notice that Turbo Edit doesn't care whether the word or phrase contains upper- or lowercase letters. (Turbo Edit also doesn't care that Fig Newtons have almost twice the calories of Oreos, but that's another story.) Any match is okay. You can change this behavior by checking the **Case** sensitive option box. When this option is selected, the search finds only words that match exactly—including the case of the letters.

To select an option box from the keyboard, press the Tab key until the blinking text cursor is in that option's check box. Then press the space bar

to *toggle*, or select, the option. To toggle an option box with the mouse, place the mouse pointer over the option and click the left mouse button.

In addition to checking for case, you can also tell Turbo Edit's search function to find only whole words. For example, suppose you're looking for the word *red* in your program. You select the **Find…** function, type *red*, and press Enter. To your surprise, the first word the computer finds is *Fred*. This is because the word *red* is part of *Fred*. If you want to find only the complete word *red*, you need to check the **Whole words only** option box. Then the Search… function ignores words that only happen to contain the letters *red*.

Now, suppose you've completed a program, and for some reason you've decided that you want to change all occurrences of the word *name* to *firstname*. You could go through the entire program, line by line, and change each occurrence of the word yourself. However, in a large program, this task would take a lot of time—not to mention make you grumpier than a hornet in a jar. Worse, you're almost certain to miss some occurrences of the word you want to change. A better way to tackle this problem is to use the **Search** menu's **R**eplace command. When you select this command, you see the dialog box shown in Fig. 15.

Fig. 15

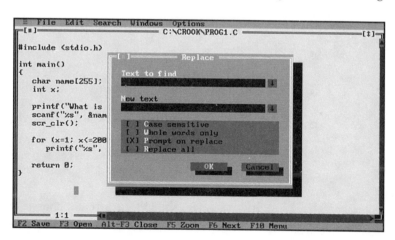

The Replace dialog box looks much like the Find dialog box, except it has two edit boxes rather than one. To use the **R**eplace command, type the word you want to find into the Text to find edit box. Press Tab to move the text cursor to the **N**ew text edit box, then type the replacement text.

You then need to select a button at the bottom of the dialog box. If you select the O**K** button, each time Turbo Edit finds the target text, it asks whether you want to change it. If you select the Replace **A**ll option, Turbo Edit does all the changes without further input from you. Often, using the O**K** button is the best way to do this type of global change. That way, you're sure that only words you want to change get changed.

To get a little experience with the change function, use it to change all occurrences of *name* in your program to *firstname*. If you need help, you can follow these steps:

1. Select the **R**eplace… entry of the **S**earch menu. The Replace dialog box appears.

2. Type the word **name** into the Text to find edit box.

3. Press the Tab key. The text cursor moves to the **N**ew text edit box.

4. Type the word **firstname**.

5. Press Tab. The text cursor moves to the **C**ase sensitive option box.

6. Press the space bar to make sure the option is selected.

7. Press the down arrow until the text cursor is on the **R**eplace all button and make sure it is selected.

8. Press Enter to select the O**K** button and change all occurrences of *name* to *firstname*.

9. Press the button for **Yes** in response to the `Replace this occurrence?` prompt. This prompt enables you to verify that you do indeed want to change all the occurrences of *name* to *firstname*. How many times do you have to tell it?

After you complete this change, your program should still run properly—for reasons you won't understand until later in this book. Whether you understand it or not, go ahead and recompile the program.

Exit Turbo Edit by pressing Alt-X. Then type **C PROG1**. When the program has been compiled and linked, you will be returned to the DOS prompt. Run the program by typing **PROG1**.

Cool, huh? The best news is that you're now ready to move on to Chapter 3, where you'll really start learning about C programming.

Summing Up

▼ You must install the Personal C Compiler before you can use it. The process of installation copies the program contents to your hard disk drive.

▼ To run Turbo Edit, type **TVEDIT** and press Enter.

▼ To load a program file, select the **O**pen option from the **File** menu.

▼ To save a program file to disk, use the **S**ave... or Save As... options from the **File** menu.

▼ To start a new program, select the **N**ew option from the **File** menu.

▼ To print a program, type **P** followed by the filename from the DOS prompt.

▼ You can view off-screen portions of a program by using the edit window's scroll bars. From your keyboard, you can scroll a program with the keyboard's Page Up, Page Down, and arrow keys.

▼ Before you can run a program, it must compiled and linked.

▼ To run a program, type the program name at the DOS command line.

▼ Using Turbo Edit, you can cut, copy, and paste text much as you would with a text editor. These editing commands are located in the Edit menu, but you can also select them using hot keys.

▼ The Turbo Edit enables you to search for and replace words or phrases in your programs. The Find... and Replace... commands are in the Search menu.

▼ To exit Turbo Edit, select the Exit entry from the File menu, or press the Alt-X hot key combination.

The next chapter covers communication with C. Well to be truthful, it is not exactly with C, but with the user of the computer. You will learn how to print information to the screen, and how to get information from the user.

CHAPTER 3

Communicating with C
(A Matter of Input and Output)

IN A NUTSHELL

▼ Understanding input and output

▼ Learning to use the **fprintf()** function

▼ Understanding variables

▼ Using the **scanf()** function

▼ Having fun with the **scr_aputs()** and sound functions

A computer wouldn't be much of a machine if you didn't have a way of getting data in and out of it. For example, let's say you want to type that letter to weird Uncle Henry. Your first task is to get the characters that make up the letter into your computer's memory where you can manipulate them. You can't just dictate the letter as you would to a secretary. Computers have terrible ears. You must use one of the computer's input devices—in this case, the keyboard—to type your letter, placing it into memory one character at a time.

When you finish typing and editing your letter, you need a way to get it out of the computer's memory so that Uncle Henry can read it. You could call Uncle Henry and have him fly in and read the letter on your computer screen, but that kind of defeats the purpose of writing a letter. Besides, Uncle Henry hates to fly, remember? You need another kind of device—an output device—to which you can send the letter and get it into a useful form. You'd probably want to use a printer, but you could also save your letter on a disk and send the disk to Uncle Henry. Then he could just load the letter into his computer's memory and read it on-screen.

The processes of moving data in and out of a computer are called, appropriately enough, *input* and *output* (or I/O, for short). There are many kinds of input and output, but you need to know only a couple to get started with the C programming language. In this chapter, you learn to retrieve data from a user and print that data on your computer's screen or on your printer.

BUZZWORD

Input Devices

Input devices, such as keyboards and mice, transfer data from you to your computer. Output devices, such as printers and monitors, transfer data from the computer back to you. Some devices, such as disk drives, are both input and output devices.

Computer Programs and I/O

(Who's the boss?)

Most input and output is controlled by the currently running program. If you load a program that doesn't use the keyboard, no matter how much you type, the program will not notice your keystrokes. Likewise, if a program wasn't designed to use your printer, you have no way of accessing the printer when running that program. Obviously, then, if it's up to a program to control your computer's input and output, every programming language must contain commands for input and output. In fact, a programming language without I/O commands would be about as useful to you as a book of matches would be to a fish. By providing commands for putting data into the computer and getting data back out again, a computer language enables you to create interactive programs.

BUZZWORD

Interactive Programs

Interactive programs enable the user and the computer to communicate with each other. For example, the computer may output a question to the user by printing the question on-screen. The user might then answer the question by typing on the keyboard.

Like any other computer language, C features several commands for controlling input and output. The `fprintf()` function, for example, enables you to make text appear on the computer's screen. To see how `fprintf()` works, bring up Turbo Edit and load the program shown in Listing 3.1.

PLAY BALL!

BUZZWORD

Functions

*Functions are small, separate units of instructions that per-
form specific duties. For example, the **fprintf()** function
sends information to an output device. Later, you will learn
how to write your own instructions.*

Listing 3.1. HITHERE1.C prints text on-screen

```c
#include <stdio.h>

int main()
{
    fprintf(stdout, "Hi, there!\n");
    fprintf(stdout, "What's a nice person like you\n");
    fprintf(stdout, "doing with a computer like this?\n");

    return 0;
}
```

The standard
output device
(the screen)

**IN SIMPLE
TERMS**

Listing 3.1 is about the simplest computer program you can
write. The **fprintf()** functions display three lines of text on-
screen.

When you run HITHERE1.C, you see a screen like this:

```
c:\crook>hithere1
Hi, there!
What's a nice person like you
doing with a computer like this?

c:\crook>
```

As you can see, each `fprintf()` command creates a single line of text on-screen. The Personal C Compiler knows that you want to send output to the screen because of the word `stdout`, which is the first piece of information (or parameter) passed to the `fprintf()` function. The word `stdout` is a short-hand term for the phrase *standard output*. It refers to the standard output device of the computer. For PC-compatible computers, `stdout` is almost always the screen.

BUZZWORD

Parameters

Parameters are the pieces of information that are passed to a function. Parameters are always separated by commas, which helps C distinguish each piece of information that a function uses.

The text the command prints is the text you use as the second piece of information to the `fprintf()` function. This text, called a *string literal*, must be enclosed in quotation marks.

BUZZWORD

String/String Literal

A string is a group of text characters. A string literal is text that you want the computer to use exactly as you type it. You tell the computer that a line of text is a string literal by enclosing the text in quotation marks.

Now, suppose you want the text printed on your printer rather than on the computer's screen? In C, this is easy to do. Just change all occurrences of the word `stdout` (which refers to the screen) to read `stdprn` (which refers to the *standard printer* device), as shown in Listing 3.2.

Listing 3.2. HITHERE2.C sends text to your printer

```
#include <stdio.h>

int main()
{                                                    Display on-screen
    fprintf(stdout, "Printing...\n");
Standard                                             Move to next line
printer
    fprintf(stdprn, "Hi, there!\n");
    fprintf(stdprn, "What's a nice person like you\n");
    fprintf(stdprn, "doing with a computer like this?\n");

    return 0;
}
```

IN SIMPLE TERMS

Listing 3.2 works much like Listing 3.1, except it sends text to your printer as well as to the screen. As before, the **fprintf()** function prints a line of text on the computer's screen. This line of text tells you that the computer is busy sending text to your printer. Finally, the last **fprintf()** functions send three lines of text to your printer.

Notice that in this program, there's an extra line that displays the word `Printing...` on-screen. Without this line, the program's user would not know what the computer was up to, except when text started appearing on the printer. Your program should always tell the user what it's doing, if it's not immediately obvious. This is especially important for any processing that takes more than a few seconds to complete. There's nothing as alarming to a computer user as watching a computer that seems to be doing nothing. You can spot alarmed computer users easily. They're the ones pounding their monitors, poking their computer's reset switches, and screaming words we can't print in this book.

The screen output for HITHERE2.C looks like this:

```
c:\crook>hithere2
Printing...

c:\crook>
```

Now you know how to use C to ask a computer user a question, which is one form of output. But how can you get the user's answer into your program? You could have the user write you a memo, but that's too slow. As you may have guessed, C has a function called scanf() that can get both numeric values and text from the user. But before you can learn about the scanf() function, you need to know about variables.

BUZZWORD

Numeric Values

Numeric values are values that can be used in mathematical operations.

Variables

(A comfy home for input)

As you've already learned, when you input data into a computer, the computer stores that data in its memory. You can think of your computer's memory as millions of little boxes, each of which holds a single value. Normally, each of these little boxes is numbered, starting at zero. The actual number of these boxes contained in your computer depends on how much memory you have installed. Fig. 1 illustrates how memory looks.

Fig.
1

```
                                    6 6
                                    4 4
                                    0 0
                                    0 0
         0 1 2 3 4 5 6 7 8          0 1
        ┌─┬─┬─┬─┬─┬─┬─┬─┬─┐  ┌─┬─┐
        └─┴─┴─┴─┴─┴─┴─┴─┴─┘..└─┴─┘
```

When you input data into your computer, a little guy named Benny grabs the data and runs away with it, giggling. Okay, I'm lying. Actually, your computer stuffs the data into one of the little boxes that make up the computer's memory. (Benny's too busy sipping beer and watching exotic dancers at Al's Drink and Drool.) But in which box should the value be stored, and how can you refer to that box in a way that makes sense within a program? You do it with variables.

Variables are memory boxes with names. Because you as the programmer supply the names, you can name your variables almost anything you want, which makes your programs easier to read and understand. (You could even name a variable Benny, although why you'd want to is a mystery.)

There are, however, some rules you must follow when creating variable names. First, a variable name must be no longer than 32 characters. Second, the name must start with a letter, but the other characters can be letters, numbers, or the underscore character (_). Because C is case-sensitive, both upper- and lowercase variable names are allowed. For example, the variable names Benny, benny, and BENNY all mean different things to C. Finally, you can't use a C keyword as a variable name.

Here are some valid variable names:

```
Total    Money_Spent    name23    AMOUNT
```

Here are some invalid variable names:

```
3456    current.balance    Date Paid    fprintf
```

Variables and *scanf()*

(A tale of two buddies)

To get input into your programs, you need to use the scanf() function. The scanf() function and variables go together like Abbott and Costello, because you must follow every scanf() function call with the name of a variable. C stores the input in the variable. Suppose you're writing a program that needs to know the number of cars in a parking garage. Suppose also that, when the user runs the program, the first thing he must do is input the current car count. This part of the program might look something like Listing 3.3.

Listing 3.3. CARS1.C gets a value from the user

```
#include <stdio.h>

int main()
{
    int cars;

    fprintf(stdout, "Please enter the number of cars\n");
    scanf("%d", &cars);
    fprintf(stdout, "You have %d cars\n", cars);

    return 0;
}
```

Integer variable declaration ——— int cars;

Ensures that information is stored in memory ——— fprintf... scanf("%d", &cars);

Replacement character for an integer

IN SIMPLE TERMS

Listing 3.3 prints a line of text on-screen, asking the user for the number of cars. The **scanf()** function allows the user to type a number on the keyboard in response to the question. The value the user types is stored in the variable **cars**. Finally, the program prints another line of text on-screen. This text is a combination of strings and the value stored in **cars**.

Start Turbo Edit and load the program for Listing 3.3 into it. Examine the code. After you have looked through the program, exit to the DOS prompt and type **C CARS1** to compile the program. To execute the program, type **CARS1**. The question displayed on the screen is your cue to input a value to the program. Type any number and press Enter. You'll see a screen that looks something like this:

```
c:\crook>cars1
Please enter the number of cars
3
You have 3 cars

c:\crook>
```

Let's examine some of these program lines again. You might notice some strange notation there. The first line

```
int cars;
```

declares a space in memory to store what the user types. This variable is referenced later in the program.

Notice the \n characters at the end of the string literal that is passed to the fprintf() function. The statement looks like this:

```
fprintf(stdout, "Please enter the number of cars\n");
```

The \n character combination (it is actually two characters) refers to a line feed. A *line feed* tells C to move the cursor to the beginning of the next line on-screen. Without these characters, the entire message would be displayed on a single line. After the first line of the screen was filled up, C would move to the second line of the screen and start printing there. It would do this until it got to the bottom of the screen.

Next, you will notice that the scanf() function takes two parameters. The first is the characters "%d". These characters tell C that it should

expect the user to enter an integer value. An integer is any whole numeric number. Examples of integers include 1, 8, 444, –23, and –99. Some numbers that are not integers are 1.5, 55.667, and –12.89.

Finally, the word `cars` following the `scanf()` function in the program is a variable name. This name is used to identify the little box in memory where your response is stored. Suppose you type the number 8 in response to the program. Your computer's memory might look something like Fig. 2. In this figure, C has assigned the variable `cars` to memory location 6 and has placed the value 8 into that location. You don't have to worry about where C puts variables in memory. C handles all that for you.

Fig. 2

```
                             c         6 6
                             a         4 4
                             r         0 0
                             s         0 0
  0 1 2 3 4 5   7 8          0 1
 ┌─┬─┬─┬─┬─┬─┬─┬─┬─┐        ┌─┬─┐
 │ │ │ │ │ │ │8│ │ │  ...   │ │ │
 └─┴─┴─┴─┴─┴─┴─┴─┴─┘        └─┴─┘
```

How about that last line in the program? Pretty fancy looking `fprintf()` function, wouldn't you say? It looks like this:

```
fprintf(stdout, "You have %d cars\n", cars)
```

This shows how powerful the `fprintf()` function can be. In this case, the `fprintf()` function displays not only string literals, but also the value stored in the variable `cars`. The way we specify the value stored in the variable `cars` is by using the `%d` code to tell C that it should expect a second parameter; in this case, the second parameter is the `cars` variable. This parameter should be displayed inside the original string. In fact, it should replace the value of the variable `cars` with the `%d` characters. Fig. 3 illustrates this replacement.

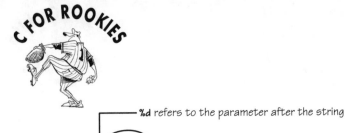

Fig.
3

%d refers to the parameter after the string

fprintf (stdout, "You have %d cars\n", cars)

As a result, the value of **cars** is inserted into the string at the location of **%d**

Numeric and String Variables

Like the `fprintf()` function, variables can be pretty flexible. Specifically, they can be of many different types. You'll learn about variable types in the next chapter, but for now, you can think of variables as being able to hold either numeric values or text. For example, run the CARS program again and this time enter a word rather than a number. When you do, the program returns a bogus value for the number of cars you entered, like this:

```
c:\crook>cars1
Please enter the number of cars
d
You have 1474 cars

c:\crook>
```

The reason for this is that the computer is stupid. If you want a specific type of input, you must tell the user exactly what you want, and take steps to make sure you check what value is entered.

PLAY BALL!

BUZZWORD

Numeric Variable/String Variable

A *numeric variable* can hold only numeric values. A *string variable* can hold only text.

You can, however, create a variable specifically for holding text. In fact, you did this in Chapter 2 when you ran the program that prints your name on-screen. To create a variable for holding text, use the word `char`

(short for character) rather than the word int when you declare the variable. Also, you must specify how long the string will be by putting the length in brackets immediately after the variable name, as shown in Listing 3.4.

Listing 3.4. CARS2.C gets text from the user

```
#include <stdio.h>

int main()
{
    char cars[255];

    fprintf(stdout, "Please enter the number of cars\n");
    scanf("%s", &cars);
    fprintf(stdout, "You have %s cars\n", cars);

    return 0;
}
```

String variable declaration ——— `char cars[255];`

Replacement character for a string ——— `scanf("%s", &cars);` / `fprintf(stdout, "You have %s cars\n", cars);`

IN SIMPLE TERMS

Like previous programs, Listing 3.4 prints a line of text to the screen, asking the user for the number of cars. Next, the **scanf()** function allows the user to type a text string on the keyboard in response to the question. Notice the use of the **%s** code to tell C that the program is expecting a string. The text the user types is stored in the variable **cars**. Finally, the program prints another line of text to the screen. This text is a combination of string literals and the value stored in cars. The maximum length of the line the user enters is 255 characters.

When you run the program in Listing 3.4, you are asked to enter the number of cars. In this case, though, whatever you type is treated as text,

not as a numeric value, which means you can type Three as well as 3.
The output of this program is shown below:

```
c:\crook>cars2
Please enter the number of cars
four
You have four cars

c:\crook>
```

Fun with *scr_aputs()* and *scanf()*

(Almost coffee break time!)

Now that you've learned a little about C input and output, how about
finishing up with a program that puts all you've learned to the test? Load
Listing 3.5 into Turbo Edit. Go ahead and compile it and run it as you
have other programs. When you run the program, it beeps and asks you
to enter your first name. After you enter your first name, the program
beeps again and asks for your last name. Finally, after you enter your last
name, the program changes the screen colors and prints a colorful message. The program's output is shown in below. (You must, of course,
have a color monitor to see the different colors.)

NOTE

If you are using the Borland or Microsoft compiler, the following program will not work because the **scr_aputs()** function is
not supported with these compilers.

Listing 3.5. CLRBEEP.C beeps and changes the text color

```
#include <stdio.h>

int main()
```

C FOR ROOKIES

```
    {
        char firstname[255];
        char lastname[255];

        fprintf(stdout, "\7");

        fprintf(stdout, "What's your first name? ");
        scanf("%s", &firstname);

        fprintf(stdout, "\7");
        fprintf(stdout, "What's your last name? ");
        scanf("%s", &lastname);

        scr_aputs("Hello There ", 4);
        fprintf(stdout, "%s %s!\n", firstname, lastname);

        return 0;
    }
```

Causes computer speaker to beep

Color code

Displays string in specified color

IN SIMPLE TERMS

Listing 3.5 first uses the **fprintf()** function to send the number 7 to the standard output device. The 7 is a code that causes the computer's speaker to emit a beep. The first **scanf()** function allows you to enter your first name, which is stored in the string variable **firstname**. After another beep, the next **scanf()** function allows you to enter your last name, which is stored in the string variable **lastname**. Finally, the **scr_aputs()** function sends text to the screen in a specified color. The first parameter to the function is the text to display, the second parameter is a number that tells what color the text should be displayed in. The final **fprintf()** function prints the first and last name as the user entered it.

The output for the program in Listing 3.5 looks like this:

```
c:\crook>clrbeep
What's your first name? Paul
What's your last name? Perry
Hello there Paul Perry!

c:\crook>
```

In CLRBEEP.C, you learn several new functions. Hopefully you noticed the `scr_aputs()` function. You are probably wandering what's going on here. The `scr_aputs()` function displays text in a specified color. You pass it the string to be displayed, and then a number that specifies what color to display the text in (see Table 3.1.).

The `fprintf()` function is passed the decimal number 7, which makes your computer's speaker beep.

PLAY BALL!

BUZZWORD

Argument

An *argument* is a value that is required by a command. For example, the text you place after a **fprintf()** function is that function's argument. Similarly, the color values you type after the **scr_aputs()** function are that command's arguments. An argument is the same thing as a parameter.

Table 3.1. Color values for the *scr_aputs* function

Code	Color
0	Black
1	Blue
2	Green

Code	Color
3	Cyan
4	Red
5	Magenta
6	Brown
7	White
8	Gray
9	Light blue
10	Light green
11	Light cyan
12	Light red
13	Light magenta
14	Yellow
15	Bright white

Be careful not to make the text color and the background color identical. Doing so causes all screen output to appear the same color, and it's impossible to read the text. It's like writing in black ink on black paper; it just won't work.

Common Rookie Mistakes

Missing or incorrect punctuation. Novice programmers tend to overlook the importance of punctuation characters such as semicolons and commas in functions. Every character in a program is important. Be careful not to overlook any.

Misspelled variable names. Spelling a variable name incorrectly creates program bugs that are difficult to find. For example, suppose you have in your program a variable named `totalnumbers`. As you type the lines of your program, you accidentally spell this variable `TotalNumbers`. To C, `totalnumbers` and `TotalNumbers` are different variables, each with its own value.

Sloppy formatting of text output. Make sure your program's text output contains spaces where needed, and that all the text is spelled correctly. Sloppy output is the mark of an amateur.

Summing Up

▼ Input and output devices transfer data to and from a computer.

▼ Most I/O is controlled by the currently running program.

▼ The `fprintf()` function, which specifies the *stdout* output device as the first parameter, prints a line of text on-screen. This command's arguments may be string literals or variables.

▼ String literals must be enclosed in quotation marks.

▼ The `fprintf()` function, which specifies the *stdprn* output device, sends its output to a printer.

▼ You can think of the computer's memory as a series of little boxes. Each box can hold a single value.

▼ Variables are named places in memory where you can store data.

▼ Numeric variables can hold only numeric values. String variables can hold only text.

▼ The scanf() function requests input from a user. The input is stored in the variable indicated by the command.

Now that you understand basic I/O, you're ready to take a closer look at the way variables work. In the next chapter, you learn about many different types of variables and how to use them in mathematical operations.

CHAPTER 4
Crunching Numbers
(The Dreaded Math Chapter)

IN A NUTSHELL

▼ Using variables in expressions
▼ Understanding arithmetic operations
▼ Handling the order of operations
▼ Using different data types

You've probably heard that programming a computer requires lots of math. And if you're like most people, all those formulas and equations you learned in high school now look stranger than an ostrich at a square dance. Guess what? Most programs require only simple mathematical calculations—addition, subtraction, multiplication, and division—the same stuff you do every day.

Moreover, when you're writing a program, you won't have to wear down pencils adding long columns of numbers or fry your brain trying to divide 35,764 by 137. The computer can do the calculations for you. If you know how to use the basic arithmetic operations to solve simple problems, you know all the math necessary to write a computer program. Programming is more logical than mathematical; it's just a matter of common sense. (If you have trouble remembering to come in out of the rain, programming may not be for you.)

Still, you can't avoid math entirely. Heaven knows, your humble author has tried. Computers, after all, are number-crunching machines that like nothing better than spitting out the results of hundreds, thousands, or even millions of calculations. And it's up to you, the wise programmer, to give the computer the commands it needs to perform those calculations. In this chapter, you'll learn to do just that.

Variables and Math

(The astounding, uncensored story)

In Chapter 3, "Communicating with C," you learned about variables—the little boxes in memory in which your program stores numbers. Unlike a constant such as the number 3, variables can represent almost any value—except maybe the balance on my Visa card, a number so large even a computer has a tough time storing it. Variables are extremely valuable entities. Because variables represent numbers, you can use them in mathematical operations.

PLAY BALL!

BUZZWORD

Constant

A *constant* is a value that cannot be changed in your program. Numbers that you type directly into your program are constants.

For example, suppose you run a small video store, and you want to know how many tapes you have. You might think to yourself, "I've got 20 copies of *Naughty Banshees from Venus*, 50 copies of *Dances with Muskrats*, and 10 copies of *Terry Gilbert's 60-Minute Workout*. So, I've got 80 videotapes." If you want to use the computer to solve this mathematical problem, you could load the C compiler and create a program with the statement `printf("%d", 20+50+10);` inside a program. After the program is compiled and executed, the computer would print the answer: 80. Just as you learned in school, the + symbol also means addition in a computer program.

There's a better way, however, to solve the videotape problem—one that works with any number of videotapes. This new method uses variables in mathematical operations. As you've learned, you can call a variable just about anything you like. (Yes, you can even call a variable `late_for_dinner`.) Names such as `Naughty`, `Dances`, and `Terry` are completely acceptable. Beginning to see the light? Look over the TAPES1.C program that follows:

Listing 4.1. TAPES1.C adds three variables

```
#include <stdio.h>

void main()
{
    int naughty;
    int dances;
    int terry;
    int tapes;
```

Variable —— declarations

continues

63

C FOR ROOKIES

Listing 4.1. Continued

```
printf("Enter number of Naughty Banshees\n");
scanf("%d", &naughty);
```
— Newline character

```
printf("Enter number of Dances with Muskrats\n");
scanf("%d", &dances);

printf("Enter number of Terry Gilbert's Workouts\n");
scanf("%d", &terry);

tapes = naughty + dances + terry;
```
— Mathematical expression

```
printf("Total number of tapes: %d\n", tapes);

}
```

IN SIMPLE TERMS

Listing 4.1 asks how many of each of the three tapes you have in inventory. Your answers are stored in the variables **naughty, dances**, and **terry.** The program then adds these three variables and places the total in the variable **tapes.** Finally, the program prints the total number of tapes.

This program asks you how many copies you have of each videotape. As you type your answers, the computer zaps those answers into the variables naughty, dances, and terry. Then, the program adds the variables and plunks the total into another variable called tapes. Finally, the program displays the number contained in tapes. Now you know two things: 1) You have 80 videotapes in your store; and 2) With movie titles like these, you'll be out of business faster than your customers can say, "*Dances with* WHAT?" The following lines of code show the output from the program in Listing 4.1:

```
c:\crook>tapes1
Enter number of Naughty Banshees
```

```
20
Enter number of Dances with Muskrats
50
Enter number of Terry Gilbert's Workouts
10
Total number of tapes: 80

c:\crook>
```

By using a program similar to this one, you can get a new tape total anytime you like. Just provide your program with new counts for each movie.

Guess what? You just used math in a computer program. It didn't hurt a bit, did it?

Beyond Addition

(More of the uncensored story)

Of course, computers can do more than add. They can perform any basic arithmetic operation. The C language even has functions for figuring out things like square roots and absolute values. If you don't know what a square root or an absolute value is, don't hit the panic button; you still won't have trouble programming your computer. Just don't plan to write an algebra tutorial anytime soon.

Let's assume that your videotape store is still thriving, even though the local chapter of Citizens Against Painfully Stupid Movies has a contract out on you. Suppose you now want to find the total cost of your inventory, as well as the average cost per tape. To find the total value of the inventory, multiply a title's price by the number of copies you own of that title. Do this calculation for each title, and then add those amounts

together to get the total cost. To find the average cost per tape, divide the total cost by the total number of tapes. You could calculate these totals using a program similar to Listing 4.2.

Listing 4.2. TAPES2.C figures the total and average costs

```c
#include <stdio.h>

void main()
{
    int number;
    int total_num_tapes;

    float price;
    float total_cost;
    float average_cost;

    printf("How much is Banshees?\n");
    scanf("%f", &price);

    printf("How many Banshees do you have?\n");
    scanf("%d", &number);

    total_num_tapes = number;
    total_cost = price * number;

    printf("How much is Dances?\n");
    scanf("%f", &price);

    printf("How many Dances do you have?\n");
    scanf("%d", &number);

    total_num_tapes = total_num_tapes + number;
    total_cost = total_cost + price * number;

    printf("How much is Terry's Workout?\n");
```

Integer variable declarations

Floating point declarations

Mathematical expressions

More mathematical expressions

```
    scanf("%f", &price);

    printf("How many Terry's do you have?\n");
    scanf("%d", &number);

    total_num_tapes = total_num_tapes + number;
    total_cost = total_cost + price * number;

    average_cost = total_cost / total_num_tapes;

    printf("\nThe total value of all tapes is: %.2f\n",
           total_cost);

    printf("The average cost is: %.2f\n", average_cost);

}
```

Even more mathematical expressions

Specifier for floating point numbers

IN SIMPLE TERMS

The program in Listing 4.2 begins declaring the variables used in the program. The **int** declaration creates storage space for an integer value, as you have already seen. The **float** type is new and stands for floating point. It allows the program to store numbers that have decimal points, such as dollar amounts. The program continues by asking for the price and quantity of the first video title. The quantity is placed in the variable **total_num_tapes**. The total cost for all tapes with that title is calculated by multiplying the price of the tape by the quantity; that total is stored in the variable **total_cost**.

Next, the program asks for the price and quantity of the second title. After the program receives that information, it adds the quantity for the second title to **total_num_tapes**,

continues

continued

which still contains the quantity for the first title. This total is the combined quantity for the first two titles. The total cost for the two titles is calculated by multiplying the second tape's price by its quantity and adding that amount to **total_cost**.

The third tape is processed the same way, then the average cost for all tapes is calculated by dividing **total_cost** by **total_num_tapes**. Finally, after printing a blank line, the program prints the total cost for all three tapes, along with the average cost per tape.

Here is the output from Listing 4.2. The numbers that appear in bold represent the values you provide.

```
c:\crook>tapes2
How much is Banshees?
29.95
How many Banshees do you have?
12
How much is Dances?
34.95
How many Dances do you have?
23
How much is Terry's Workout?
14.98
How many Terry's do you have?
8

The total value of all tapes is: 1283.09
The average cost is: 29.84

c:\crook>
```

This program is a bit longer than the first one, but it still uses only basic arithmetic. It's longer because it performs more calculations than the first example.

What's going on here? This program first asks you for the price and quantity of each tape you have in stock. The program then calculates the total cost of all the tapes in your store, as well as your average cost per tape. If you look at the program carefully, you'll see something strange about total_num_tapes. Specifically, what the heck does the line total_num_tapes = total_num_tapes + number do? How can the same variable be on both sides of an equation? Why do I keep asking these dumb questions?

First, you have to stop thinking that the equal sign (=) always means *equals*. It doesn't. In arithmetic operations, the equal sign actually means "takes the value of "—which is the meaning it has in C programming when it is used as an *assignment operator*.

You also must understand that the C compiler checks your statements from right to left. So, in Listing 4.2 total_num_tapes and number are added first, and then the result is assigned back to total.num.tapes.

BUZZWORD

Assignment Operator

An *assignment operator* is used to assign a value to a variable. In C, the assignment operator is an equal sign (**=**), but other computer languages may use different assignment operators. In Pascal, for example, the assignment operator is a colon followed by an equal sign (:=).

Confused? How about an example? Suppose total_num_tapes is equal to 7 and number is equal to 3. When the computer sees the line total_num_tapes = total_num_tapes + number, it adds 7 to 3 and pops the value 10 into total_num_tapes. Using this method, you can add values to

a variable that already holds a value. You'll do this often in your programs.

As you can see, a C program uses an asterisk (*) to represent multiplication, not an x as you might expect. Division is represented by the slash character (/) because the computer keyboard doesn't have a division symbol. You could try painting a division symbol on one of your keys, but you'll still have to use the slash character in your programs.

Table 4.1 displays all the C arithmetic operators. Table 4.2 shows the results of various mathematical operations.

Table 4.1. The arithmetic operators in C

Operator	Name	Use
+	Addition	Sum values
−	Subtraction	Subtract values
*	Multiplication	Multiply values
/	Division	Divide values
%	Modulus	Determine the remainder of division

Table 4.2. The results of some arithmetic operations

Operation	Result
5+8	13
12-7	5

Operation	Result
3*6	18
9/3	3
10%3	1

TIP

The modulus operator is rather unique in that it returns the result of the remainder in a division operation. For example, 7 divided by 3 equals 2, remainder 1. The expression **7%3** returns the value **1**.

Order of Operations

(Me first! Me first!)

Another rather curious line in Listing 4.2 is `total_cost = total_cost + price * number`. This program line is similar to the line that calculates the total number of tapes, but it contains both an addition and multiplication operation. So it's time to discuss the important topic of *operator precedence* or, as it's more commonly known, the order of operations.

If you add `total_cost` to `price` and multiply the sum by `number`, you get an incorrect result. Operator precedence dictates that all multiplication must take place before any addition. So in the preceding line, `total_cost` is calculated by first multiplying `price` times `number`, then adding that product to `total_cost`.

Don't forget about operator precedence; if you do, your calculations won't be accurate and your programs won't run correctly. Not adhering to the rules of operator precedence can also affect your home life: broken programs make for grumpy programmers, and grumpy programmers are no fun to have around.

The order of operations for C is multiplication, division, modulus, and finally, addition and subtraction. This order is summarized in Table 4.3.

Table 4.3. Operator precedence in C

Order	Operator	Name
2	* / %	Multiplication, division, and modulus
3	+ −	Addition and subtraction

You can change operator precedence by using parentheses. For example, suppose you wanted the addition in the line `total_cost = total_cost + price * number` to be calculated before the multiplication. You could rewrite the line as `total_cost = (total_cost + price) * number`. Any operation enclosed in parentheses is performed first. Consequently, `total_cost` and `price` are added first, and the sum is then multiplied by `number`.

Operations with the same precedence level are evaluated on a left-to-right basis. To see what this means, suppose a line reads `total_cost = number + price - discount`. The order of operations is carried out from left to right. Therefore, the value of `number` is added to the value of `price`, then `discount` is subtracted from the result of `number + price`.

At first glance the modulus operator may appear to be an esoteric feature that only mathematicians and physicists would use. Actually, it is rather

practical and helpful. Suppose you want to convert a number from just seconds to minutes and seconds. If you enable the user to enter the number of seconds into a variable named `secs`, a line such as `min = secs / 60` returns the number of whole minutes. To find the number of remaining seconds, use a line such as `left = secs % 60`.

For example, if the user enters the number 234, the line `min = secs / 60` assigns the variable `min` with the value of 3. Then, the line `left = secs % 60` results in the number 54; and 234 seconds is the same as 3 minutes and 54 seconds.

TIP

When writing a program line that contains many arithmetic operations, you may want to use parentheses to more clearly indicate the order of operation. For example, the formula

```
total_cost = total_cost + (price * number)
```

is easier to read than the original formula

```
total_cost = total_cost + price * number
```

Both formulas, however, yield the same result.

Data Types

(What's a nice integer like you doing in a program like this?)

You'll be happy to know you're almost finished with the math stuff. You only have to explore one more topic before you move on: data types. You've already had a little experience with data types, but you probably didn't realize it at the time.

CHAPTER 4

When you used numeric variables and string variables, you were using variables of two different data types. Numeric variables can hold only numbers, and string variables can hold only text strings. What you haven't learned is that numeric variables can be divided into many other data types, including integers, long integers, single-precision, and double-precision.

Although numeric variables can hold only numbers and string variables can hold only text strings, that doesn't mean a string variable can't hold a character that represents a number. For example, when assigned to a numeric variable, the number 3 represents a value that can be used in arithmetic operations. However, the *character* 3 assigned to a string variable is just a text character—no different from any other text character such as A or Z. Although a string variable can hold number characters, those characters cannot be used directly in mathematical operations.

Until now, you've been concerned only with giving your numeric variables appropriate names; you haven't worried about what type of value they would hold. You could ignore a variable's data type because C can determine data types on its own. But what if you want to be sure that a variable always contains a certain type of data, no matter what type of assignment operation it's involved in? For example, what if you want to add two real numbers, but you want to store the result as an integer? What are real numbers and integers, anyway?

An *integer* is any whole number, such as 23, 76, –65, or 1,200. Notice that none of these numbers contain a decimal portion. Notice also that none of them are smaller than –32,768 or greater than 32,767. A C integer must fall into this range. The reason that integer variable must be in this range is because of the amount of memory used to store the value.

What if you have to use a number that doesn't fit into the integer range? You can use a long integer. A *long integer* resembles an integer in that it can hold only a whole number. However, the range of a long integer is much larger: –2,147,483,648 to 2,147,483,647, to be exact. Unless you're trying to calculate the national debt or count the number of times Elizabeth Taylor has been married, you're not likely to need values larger than these. The declaration for a long integer uses the word long. An example is `long BigNumber`. This declares a variable named `BigNumber` of type `long`.

Numbers that contain a decimal portion are called *floating point* or *real* numbers. Like integers, they come in two flavors. The first type is accurate down to six decimal places (for example, 34.875637) and declared as a `float`. The other type is accurate down to 14 decimal places (for example, 657.36497122357638) and is declared as type `double`. Real numbers in C can be very tiny or incredibly large.

CAUTION

When writing a program, you may be tempted to make all your integer variables long integers and all your floating point number variables double-precision. When you do this, you no longer have to worry about whether your values go out of range. However, this technique has two drawbacks. First, long integers and double-precision floating point numbers take up more memory than their smaller counterparts. Second, your computer takes longer to access and manipulate these larger values, so using them can significantly slow down your programs. Use long integers and double-precision values only when you really need them.

As you have seen, the C programming language requires that all variables be declared before they are used. The declaration tells the compiler what type of information will be stored in this variable. You have seen statements like:

```
int naughty;
int dances;
int terry;
int tapes;
```

Each of these statements declares a variable. However, it seems repetitive to use a type of variable multiple times (as is done with `int` in the preceding example.) Fortunately, there is a way to simplify the programmer's life. The solution that C provides is to specify multiple variable names within a single variable declaration. For example, the previous declarations could be rewritten in one line like this:

```
int naughty, dances, terry, tapes;
```

Besides allowing you to type fewer instructions, this declaration is easier to read. It is one of the features of C that programmers like.

NOTE

> Like a variable, a constant has a data type. The difference is that the data type is implicit. For example, 10 is an integer, 23.7564 is a floating point number, and "Alexander" is a string. You can tell what the data type is just by looking at the value, and so can C.

Listing 4.3 is a revised version of Listing 4.2 that has a single variable declaration for each variable type. This program works the same as the original; the only difference is that variables are declared in multiples.

Listing 4.3. TAPES3.C uses specific data types

```
#include <stdio.h>

void main()
{
    int number, total_num_tapes;
```
Multiple integer variable declarations

Multiple floating ——— `float price, total_cost, average_cost;`
point declarations

```c
float price, total_cost, average_cost;

printf("How much is Banshees?\n");
scanf("%f", &price);

printf("How many Banshees do you have?\n");
scanf("%d", &number);

total_num_tapes = number;
total_cost = price * number;

printf("How much is Dances?\n");
scanf("%f", &price);

printf("How many Dances do you have?\n");
scanf("%d", &number);

total_num_tapes = total_num_tapes + number;
total_cost = total_cost + price * number;

printf("How much is Terry's Workout?\n");
scanf("%f", &price);

printf("How many Terry's do you have?\n");
scanf("%d", &number);

total_num_tapes = total_num_tapes + number;
total_cost = total_cost + price * number;

average_cost = total_cost / total_num_tapes;

printf("\nThe total value of all tapes is: %.2f\n",
        total_cost);

printf("The average cost is: %.2f\n", average_cost);

}
```

Except for the modified variable declaration, the program is exactly the same as Listing 4.2.

CAUTION

You want to be careful when assigning variables of two different types. For example, suppose there are two variables, declared like this:

```
int integer;
float floating;
```

If the integer variable is assigned a number like 10 and the floating variable a number like 55.25, the program can include a statement like:

```
integer = floating;
```

However, there is a problem because the variable integer cannot store the value 55.25. What the compiler will do is truncate (a big word meaning "chop off") the decimal part of the number (the part of the number on the right side of the decimal point.) Therefore, after the previous assignment statement the variable integer equals 55.

If you try to go the other way and assign the integer to the floating point number, such as

```
floating = integer;
```

the compiler will have no problem because the floating point number will now contain the number 10.00 (notice the decimal point).

You always have to be aware of the conversion issues covered. Stuffy technical books sometimes call the conversion process type conversion. However, it is nothing to be too concerned with in beginning programming.

There is one other unique aspect about Listings 4.2 and 4.3 that we should examine. You may have been puzzled by this statement:

```
printf("The average cost is: %.2f\n", average_cost);
```

The confusing part is the `%.2f\n`. The first part of that—`%.2f`—tells the `printf()` function to display a floating point number with two decimal places. If it is rewritten as `%f`, it should remind you of `%d`, which is used to display integer numbers. The `%f` tells `printf()` to display a floating point number. The `.2` in the middle of the `%f` tells the `printf()` function to display the first two decimal places of the floating point number. If the program had a statement like `%.4f`, it would tell `printf()` to display four decimal places. Finally, the `\n` (as you have already seen) moves the cursor to the beginning of the next line. Looking at it step by step makes it easier, don't you think?

Common Rookie Mistakes

Misinterpreting the equal sign. When used in arithmetic operations in C, the equal sign (=) means *takes the value of*. It is an assignment operator.

Using the wrong symbol for an arithmetic operator. The symbol for multiplication in C is the asterisk (*), not an x.

Overlooking operator precedence. If you want to be sure your formulas yield correct results, double-check the formula's order of operations. Better still, use parentheses in your formulas to ensure that all arithmetic operations are completed in the order you expect.

Using the wrong data type. Remember that integers cannot hold values outside the range –32,768 to 32,767. If you try to assign a value outside this range to an integer variable, you'll get unexpected results. The other data types also have limited ranges. However, their ranges are so much

larger than the integer's that you're not likely to run into values too small or too large for them.

Summing Up

▼ Computer programming requires more logic than math. However, you can't avoid some mathematical operations in your programs.

▼ Variables can hold any value you assign to them, whereas constants never change. Because variables can change value in your programs, you can use them to represent numbers whose values you don't know ahead of time.

▼ You can perform all normal arithmetic operations with C, including addition (+), subtraction (-), multiplication (*), and division (/). The other operation available is modulus (%).

▼ When used in formulas, the equal sign (=) acts as an assignment operator.

▼ All formulas in C follow the standard rules of operator precedence (order of operation).

▼ Variables and constants in a C program can be one of many data types, including integer, long integer, floating point, double, and string.

You've learned a lot about using math and data types in C. You'll run into these topics again in this book, but the worst is behind you. In the next chapter you'll take a closer look at the string data type, which gives you many ways to manipulate text in your programs.

CHAPTER 5
Working with Text
(A Frank Textual Discussion)

IN A NUTSHELL

▼ Joining strings
▼ Using string lengths
▼ Handling substrings
▼ Converting strings and numbers

Pictures of bathing beauties or well-oiled hunks may be more fun to look at than a screen full of words and numbers; the simple truth, however, is that most information displayed on your computer screen is in text form. This fact separates computer users into two groups: those who would rather hang out at the beach, and those who understand that computers are designed to help humans deal with large amounts of information—information usually presented in text form.

Because text displays are so important in computing, C has a number of functions and commands that manipulate text. These functions enable you to join two or more strings into one, find the length of a string, extract a small portion of a string, or convert numbers to strings or strings to numbers. In this chapter, you'll learn to use many of C's string-handling functions.

The Full Scoop on Strings

Up to this point, the term *string* has been used rather loosely. A string is actually just a group of characters. The word "beetlejuice" or the expressions "How's it going?" and "Give me five!" are all examples of strings.

To use a string, you must tell the C compiler how big you expect the string to be. The size of the string is specified when the variable is declared. For example,

```
char string1[25];
```

declares a string (named `string1`) that can be a maximum of 25 characters long. The keyword `char` stands for character; you pronounce it like charcoal, but shorter.

You might ask, "What do I do if I want a string with a maximum length of one?" No problem; you can specify a string with length of one like this:

```
char string1[1];
```

But if you only want a length of one, you don't have to specify a size at all; C assumes you want a string of one character. The simplified version that creates a character variable with the name looks like this:

```
char ch;
```

At this point, however, you no longer have a string declaration; you have a character declaration. Remember, a string is a group of characters. A single character is called, well, a single character. You probably won't find yourself using characters as much as you use strings, but it's nice to know some of the shortcuts C lets us take.

When you specify the size of the string, you can always tell C to reserve more space than you plan on using. In fact, it's better to do that than not allocate enough space in the first place.

NOTE

Always make sure enough space is reserved for a string. C does not keep track of how much memory has been reserved for a string, and if you try to store text in a string larger than the available memory, memory space gets written over. Once memory space starts getting written over, your program may stop working—not something you want to happen.

Another neat feature of C you can take advantage of is the ability to declare the contents of the string at the time the string is declared. It looks like this:

```
char name[] = "Thomas Edison was here";
```

83

This statement assigns the string name with the phrase Thomas Edison was here. Notice that no size was specified inside the square brackets. C is smart enough to count the length of the string (22 characters long) and reserve enough memory to put the specified string in. The above declaration does not stop you from using a statement like this:

```
char name[35] = "Thomas Edison was here";
```

This time, C will reserve 35 characters in memory rather than just the 22 for the string.

At this point, you are probably pretty excited about strings and want to start using them. So let's take a look at some functions your C programs can use to manipulate strings.

Getting String Data

So far, you have seen the printf() function used to display strings and the scanf() function used to input strings from the user. These functions work fine. However, there is actually another way. Isn't there always?

The other functions available are the gets() and puts() string functions. To get input from the user and store it in a string named str, use the following statement:

```
gets(str);
```

To display the string str on-screen, use this statement:

```
puts(str);
```

These functions carry out the same results as printf() and scanf().
However, there is an exception: If you have to pass values to be
displayed on-screen, you can't use the puts() function. For example,
if you use a statement like

```
printf("The string %s is %d characters long", str, 25);
```

you will not find the puts() function useful. But if you're not doing multiple character replacements, the function will work fine.

The advantage of using puts() over printf() is you don't have to remember a long list of arguments to pass to the function. For example,
instead of typing

```
printf("%s", str);
```

you can simply use the statement

```
puts(str);
```

The same goes with gets(). Rather than

```
scanf("%s", &str);
```

you can use

```
gets(str);
```

I'll bet you like this. By using gets() and puts(), you also save your tired
fingers from extra typing. That alone is enough incentive for most computing professionals to use puts() and gets() over printf() and scanf()
whenever possible.

Joining Strings

(Till death do they part)

You'll often have two or more strings in your programs that you must combine into one. For example, you may have a user's first name and last name in two separate strings. To get the user's entire name into a single string, you have to *concatenate* (join together end-to-end) the two strings. Use C's concatenation function for this string-handling task. To join two strings, for example, type the following:

```
strcat(string1, string2);
```

PLAY BALL!

BUZZWORD

Concatenation

Concatenation is the process of joining two or more strings end-to-end to create one large string. C performs concatenation with the **strcat()** *function.*

The `strcat()` function works by sticking `string2` to the end of `string1`. After the function is executed, `string1` contains its own contents as well as the contents of `string2` appended to the end of it.

To see how all this works, look at Listing 5.1.

NOTE

If you are using Turbo C++ or Borland C++, make sure you add the following line to the program:

```
#include <string.h>
```

It should appear directly underneath the line that reads

```
#include <stdio.h>
```

The line is required to include extra function declarations, which are required by these compilers. If you are using the Borland compilers, this change will be required for all the programs in this chapter.

Listing 5.1. NAME1.C joins two strings

```c
#include <stdio.h>

int main()
{
    char first[50];
    char last[50];

    printf("Enter your first name: ");
    scanf("%s", first);

    printf("Enter your last name: ");
    scanf("%s", last);

    strcat(first, " ");
    strcat(first, last);

    printf("Your full name is: %s\n", first);

    return 0;

}
```

Add the last name to the first name, including the space between them ——— strcat(first, last);

strcat(first, " "); ——— Add a space to the end of the first name

IN SIMPLE TERMS

Listing 5.1 asks you to enter your first and last names. The names are stored in the variables **first** and **last**, respectively. A blank space (" ") is appended to the end of the first string.

continues

continued

You then join the two strings using the concatenation function, and the result is stored in the string variable first. Finally, after printing a blank line, the program prints your full name on-screen.

When you compile the program by typing **C NAME1** from the DOS command prompt, and then run the NAME1 program, you are asked to type your first name and then your last name. The program then prints your full name on-screen.

Your name being displayed isn't what makes this program interesting—you already know how to use a `printf()` function to display output. What's interesting is that the final output is in a single string, `first`. This single string is created by using C's concatenation function to join the two original strings into one resulting string.

Listing 5.1 delivers the following output:

```
c:\crook>name1
Enter your first name: Freddy
Enter your last name: Kruger
Your full name is: Freddy Kruger

c:\crook>
```

This program also works if you type your first and last name on one line. For example, when the program asks for your first name, you could type Freddy Kruger, and the program will respond with Your full name is: Freddy Kruger. However, it truncates three or more names on the first line that are separated by two or more spaces.

The Length of a String

(The long and short of it)

Every string has a length. It is always the number that is specified in the string declaration. For example,

```
char first[50];
```

declares a string variable 50 characters long. This is the maximum length that a string can be. The actual string that is stored inside the variable can be any length up to 50 characters. The actual text held within a string is variable and can be any length up to the maximum that you define.

It is important to specify a string length that won't be too big (because it wastes valuable memory) or too small (because it might not hold the entire string).

If a string declaration is not large enough, the string manipulation functions (like the strcat() function) will try to carry out their normal operations, even if enough space is not available. The result is the string functions will overwrite memory that does not belong to the string. Because of the way memory is organized, this may or may not effect other variables in a program. However, you never want to take a chance.

TIP

Always make sure that enough space is allocated for a string variable when it is declared. Not allocating enough space can cause serious problems.

Sometimes in your programs you may need to know the length of a string. For example, you might want to calculate the position of a string

on-screen if the position of one string depends on where a previous string ends. To find the length of a string variable, use C's `strlen()` function, as in the following:

```
length = strlen(string1);
```

Here, the function's single argument, `string1`, is the string for which you want the length. The `strlen()` function returns the length of the string as a numerical value that can be used anywhere you can use a numerical value.

The length returned by `strlen()` is not the length that the string was originally declared to be. It is the actual length of the text that is stored inside the string. For example, suppose you declare a variable like this:

```
char car[35] = "Honda";
```

Although you have declared the string to hold 35 characters, the statement

```
length = strlen(car);
```

returns the number 5.

Arguments are the values passed to a function within parentheses. For example, in the above expression, the variable `car` is called an argument.

PLAY BALL!

BUZZWORD

Function Call/Return Value

A *function call* in C consists of a function name followed by parentheses that contain the function's arguments. A function call usually returns a single value. A *return value* is a value that can be assigned to a variable. It is much like evaluating a variable and testing it for a value.

In the case of the **strlen()** function, the return value is the length of the string passed to the function as the argument.

Listing 5.2 is a revised version of Listing 5.1 that uses the strlen() function.

Listing 5.2. NAME2.C joins two strings and displays their lengths

```c
#include <stdio.h>

int main()
{
    char first[255], last[255];
    int length;

    printf("Enter your first name: ");
    scanf("%s", first);

    printf("Enter your last name: ");
    scanf("%s", last);

    strcat(first, " ");
    strcat(first, last);

    printf("Your full name is: %s\n", first);

    length = strlen(first);   ———————————  strlen() returns
                                            the length of a
                                            string
    printf("The length of your name is %d", length);

    return 0;

}
```

IN SIMPLE TERMS

Listing 5.2 is similar to Listing 5.1 except for several extra lines. The first new line is an integer variable declaration at the beginning of the program. The end of the program also has several new lines. You will see a line that gets the length of the string variable first and stores it in the integer variable length. Finally, the last line displays the value of length.

The following is the output from Listing 5.2:

```
c:\crook>name2
Enter your first name: James
Enter your last name: Bond
Your full name is: James Bond
The length of your name is 10

c:\crook>
```

TIP

In Listing 5.2, you don't have to use the variable length. You could rewrite the last two lines as one, like this:

```
printf("The length of your name is %d", strlen(first));
```

This method demonstrates how you can use functions in the same way you use numbers or numeric variables.

Extracting a Substring

(Bits and pieces)

Just as you can concatenate strings to create a larger string, you can separate strings into smaller strings called *substrings*. The C language has two special string-handling functions, strncpy() and strcpy(), created especially to extract whatever portion of a string you need.

PLAY BALL!

BUZZWORD

Substring

A *substring* is a portion of a larger string. For example, the string Twitdum is a substring of Seymour Twitdum.

The strncpy() function returns a specified number of characters in a string beginning with the leftmost, or first, character of the string.

To use strncpy(), you might type commands such as the following:

```
char src[25];
char dest[25];

strncpy(dest, src, 7);
```

This function call has three arguments. The first argument is the destination string to store the resulting string; the second argument is the string you want to cut from; the third argument is the maximum number of characters, counting from the first character in the string, to include in the substring. So, the example

```
strncpy(string1, string2, 7);
```

returns the first seven characters of the variable string2. If string2 was the phrase Yo ho ho and a bottle of rum, string2 would return the string Yo ho h.

The strcpy() function copies the entire contents of one string to another string. It is similar to strncpy(), except it does not take an integer specifying the maximum number of characters to copy. It copies the entire string. Therefore, the statement

```
strcpy(string1, string2);
```

assigns the contents of string2 to string1. If string2 is the phrase C is way cool!, the call to strcpy() would assign the phrase C is way cool! to string1.

C FOR ROOKIES

To get a little practice with substrings, try the program in Listing 5.3. When you run the program, you are asked to enter a string. Type anything you like, as long as the text is at least seven characters long and doesn't contain any words that make people blush. After you enter the string, the program extracts several substrings and displays them on-screen.

Listing 5.3. STRING1.C displays substrings

```
#include <stdio.h>

    char string1[255] = "";
    char string2[255] = "";
    char string3[255] = "";
```
String declarations assign a length of zero to the string

```
int main()
{

    printf("Enter a string: ");
    scanf("%s", string1);

    strcpy(string2, string1);
    strncpy(string3, string1, 5);

    printf("A copy of the string is %s\n", string2);
    printf("The first five characters are %s\n", string3);

    return 0;
}
```
strcpy() and **strncpy()** *copy a string*

IN SIMPLE TERMS

Listing 5.3 asks the user to input a string. The program then takes the user's string, which is stored in the string variable **string1,** and uses the string-handling functions **strcpy()** and **strncpy()** to extract two substrings. These substrings are

stored in the variables **string2** and **string3,** respectively. Finally, after printing a blank line, the program displays the substrings.

Here's the output for Listing 5.3:

```
c:\crook>string1
Enter a string: Supercalifragilisticexpialidocious
A copy of the string is Supercalifragilisticexpialidocious
The first five characters are Super

c:\crook>
```

NOTE

When you run the program in Listing 5.3, try entering a string that's less than five characters in length. Because the **strcpy()** and **strncpy()** string-handling functions assume a string length of at least five characters, you might expect the program to drop dead if you give it a string shorter than it expects. However, the output below shows what really happens. C's functions are smart little devils. If you give them values that don't make sense, they can usually figure out how to handle the situation. Despite C's cleverness, you should watch out for this kind of error. The following output shows what happens if you enter a string with fewer than five characters:

```
c:\crook>string1
Enter a string: rat
A copy of the string is rat
The first five characters are rat

c:\crook>
```

Finding Substrings

(A textual scavenger hunt)

Now that you know how to extract a substring from a larger string, you may wonder how you can find the exact substring you want. Suppose, for example, you have a string containing a list of names, and you want to find the name Twitdum. The function strstr() was created for just this task. (Well, actually, it was created to find any string, not just Twitdum.)

The strstr() function enables you to find the first occurrence of a substring by providing the function with the source string (the string to search through) as well as the substring for which to search. For example, the following example returns a *pointer* to the substring Twitdum in string1:

```
str = strstr(string1, "Twitdum")
```

You may have heard that pointers are a difficult concept to grasp. Well, the following brief explanation will put an end to that myth. A pointer to a string is different than a regular string. Instead of actually containing a string, a pointer has a memory address which points to where the string is stored in memory (see Fig. 1). A pointer declaration looks like this:

```
char *ptr;
```

As you can see, declaring a pointer to a string is different than declaring a string.

When a string is declared, memory is reserved for the string to be stored in. When a pointer is declared, only enough memory is reserved for a number that points to the string. The number used to point to the string is used internally by C and shouldn't concern you.

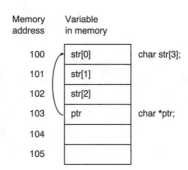

Fig. 1

Memory address / Variable in memory

100	str[0]	char str[3];
101	str[1]	
102	str[2]	
103	ptr	char *ptr;
104		
105		

The program in Listing 5.4 demonstrates how this substring-search and pointer-declaration stuff works. The program requires no input; just run it and compare its output with the program listing.

Listing 5.4. FIND1.C finds substrings

```
#include <stdio.h>

char string1[] = "SmithTwitdumFreemanTwitdumRothTwitdum";

int main()
{
    char *ptr;

    ptr = strstr(string1, "Twitdum");
    printf("The first occurence of 'Twitdum' is %s\n", ptr);

    ptr = strstr(ptr, "Freeman");
    printf("The first occurence of 'Freeman' is %s\n", ptr);

    ptr = strstr(ptr, "Roth");
    printf("The first occurence of 'Roth' is %s\n", ptr);

    return 0;
}
```

The list of names

strstr() finds the substrings

**IN SIMPLE
TERMS**

Listing 5.4 sets the string variable **string1** to a list of names.
It also declares a pointer to a string, called **ptr**. Then the
program uses the **strstr()** function to find the position of
the first occurrence of the substring **Twitdum.** A pointer to
the substring is returned, and the **printf()** function is used to
display the string starting at the substring. Next, the
strstr() function is used to return a pointer to the string
Freeman and the resulting string is displayed on-screen with
printf(). The occurrence of the substring **Roth** is located and
displayed in the same way.

Here is the output from the program in Listing 5.4:

```
c:\crook>find1
The first occurence of 'Twitdum' is
TwitdumFreemanTwitdumRothTwitdum
The first occurence of 'Freeman' is FreemanTwitdumRothTwitdum
The first occurence of 'Roth' is RothTwitdum

c:\crook>
```

Another way to use the string functions presented in this chapter is to
allow the user to enter strings, and then use the string functions on the
data which was entered by the user. Listing 5.5 is a program that asks
you to type a string and a substring. It then displays the substring along
with the rest of the string.

Listing 5.5. FIND2.C searches for a substring inside a string

```
#include <stdio.h>

int main()
```

Pointer declaration ——

The **strstr()** function finds one string inside another

```
{
    char str1[80], str2[80];
    char *ptr;

    printf("Enter a string: ");
    scanf("%s", &str1);

    printf("Enter string to locate in the first: ");
    scanf("%s", &str2);

    ptr = strstr(str1, str2);
    printf("'%s' in '%s'\nRest of string: %s\n", str1, str2,
ptr);

    return 0;
}
```

IN SIMPLE TERMS

The first two lines of Listing 5.5 declare two string variables and one pointer to a string variable. The program asks for a string to search. It then asks for a substring to find. It uses the **strstr()** function to locate the substring inside the string and then displays the rest of the string, starting at the substring.

Here is the output from Listing 5.5:

```
c:\crook>find2
Enter a string: international
Enter string to locate in the first: nation
'international' in 'nation'
Rest of string: national

c:\crook>
```

Listing 5.5 is the most complicated program you've confronted. Study it carefully to be sure you understand the way the function determines the location of the substring in the string. When you understand this program, you're well on your way to becoming a C programmer.

Changing Case

(A capital idea)

As you know, alphabetic characters can be either uppercase or lowercase. Sometimes, you might want your strings to be displayed all in one case or the other. To change all characters in a string to either uppercase or lowercase, use C's handy `strupr()` and `strlwr()` functions.

To see how `strupr()` and `strlwr()` work, try the program in Listing 5.6.

Listing 5.6. CASES.C displays strings in uppercase and lowercase

```c
#include <stdio.h>

int main()
{
   char string1[80];

   printf("Enter a string: ");
   scanf("%s", string1);

   printf("Normal: %s\n", string1);

   printf("UPPERCASE: %s\n", strupr(string1));

   printf("lowercase: %s\n", strlwr(string1));

   return 0;
}
```

                                                    ┌──────── Convert string to
                                                    │   uppercase
                                                    ┌──────── Convert string to
                                                    │   lowercase

IN SIMPLE TERMS

Listing 5.6 accepts a string from the user. It then displays the string as it was entered by the user, then in all upper-case, and finally in all lowercase.

When you compile the example program by typing **C CASES** from DOS and then run CASES.EXE, be sure the word you enter as your string includes both uppercase and lowercase letters. After you type the string, the program displays the word the way you typed it, followed by the same word in uppercase and then in lowercase letters. The following is the output for Listing 5.6:

```
c:\crook>cases
Enter a string: WildCat
Normal: WildCat
UPPERCASE: WILDCAT
lowercase: wildcat

c:\crook>
```

Common Rookie Mistakes

Formatting strings improperly. When concatenating strings, it's easy to forget that you might need to separate the strings with some sort of delimiter. For example, when joining a first name to a last name, you'll end up with a string like `GaryGilbert` if you forget to add a space between the two names.

Assuming a specific string length. As you saw in the second output example for Listing 5.3 (in which a string with fewer than five characters was entered), you must be careful when you make assumptions about a string's length. This fact is particularly important to remember when the string is being entered by the user.

Using a C keyword or function name as a variable name. If you get strange errors in your program, check the line in question for invalid variable names. You might think `char` makes a perfectly good string name, but C will complain vociferously because `char` is the name of a C keyword.

Placing function arguments in the wrong order. When you call a function such as `strstr()`, be certain that you have the function's arguments in the right order. A function call such as

```
ptr = strstr(string, substring, 5)
```

works just fine, but the function call

```
ptr = strstr(5, substring, string)
```

stops a C compiler dead in its tracks.

Summing Up

▼ You can use the `gets()` and `puts()` functions as replacements to the `scanf()` and `printf()` functions for getting and displaying strings.

▼ You can use the `strcat()` function to join strings together. This process is called concatenation.

▼ The `strcpy()` function can be used with strings to set a string variable to a specific string value.

▼ The length of a string is the number of characters contained in the string. A null string contains no characters and so has a length of `0`.

▼ The `strlen()` function returns, as a numerical value, the length of a string.

▼ A substring is a portion of a larger string.

▼ The functions `strncpy()` and `strcpy()` allow you to extract substrings from other strings.

▼ The function `strstr()` returns the position of a substring within a string.

▼ You can use the functions `strlwr()` and `strupr()` to convert strings to lowercase and uppercase, respectively.

CHAPTER 6

Making Decisions

(Or How to Really Put Your Computer to Work)

IN A NUTSHELL

▼ Using branching to change program flow
▼ Learning about the **if** and **else** statements
▼ Understanding relational operators
▼ Working with logical operators

In previous chapters, you learned a lot about the way C works. You now know how to type programs, how to input and output data, how to perform mathematical operations, and how to handle strings. But these techniques are merely the building blocks of a program. To use these building blocks in a useful way, you have to understand how computers make decisions.

In this chapter, you learn how your programs can analyze data in order to decide what parts of your program to execute. Until now, your programs have executed their statements in strict sequential order, starting with the first line and working, line by line, to the end of the program. Now it's time to learn how you can control your *program flow*—the order in which the statements are executed—so that you can do different things based on the data your program receives.

PLAY BALL!

BUZZWORD

Program Flow
Program flow is the order in which a program executes its statements. Most program flow is sequential, meaning that the statements are executed one by one in the order in which they appear in the program. However, there are C commands that make your program jump forward or backward, skipping over program code not currently required. These commands are said to control the program flow.

If the idea of computers making decisions based on data seems a little strange, think about how you make decisions. For example, suppose you're expecting an important letter. You go out to your mailbox and look inside. Based on what you find, you choose one of two actions:

▼ If there's mail in the mailbox, you take it into the house.

▼ If there's no mail in the mailbox, you complain about the postal system.

In either case, you've made a decision based on whether there is mail in the mailbox. This is called *conditional branching*.

Computers use this same method to make decisions (except they never complain and they don't give a darn how late your mail is). You will see the word *if* used frequently in computer programs. Just as you might say to yourself, "If the mail is in the mailbox, I'll bring it in," a computer also uses *if* to decide what action to take.

Program Flow and Branching

(A digital road map)

Program flow is the order in which a program executes its code. Your programs so far in this book have had sequential program flow, starting at the first line of the program and working down to the last line. Truth is, almost all program code executes sequentially. However, virtually every program reaches a point where a decision must be made about a piece of data. The program must then analyze the data, decide what to do about it, and jump to the appropriate section of code. This decision-making process is as important to computer programming as pollen is to a bee. Virtually no useful programs can be written without it.

When a program breaks the sequential flow and jumps, or branches, to a new section of code, it is called *branching*. When this branching is based on a decision, the program is performing *conditional branching*. When no decision-making is involved and the program always branches when it encounters a branching instruction, the program is performing *unconditional branching*. Unconditional branching is rarely used in modern programs, so this chapter deals primarily with conditional branching.

Unconditional branching occurs whenever a particular decision is always the same. For example, driving to the store and taking the exact same route every single time is an example of unconditional branching.

C FOR ROOKIES

PLAY BALL!

BUZZWORD

Unconditional and Conditional Branching
Unconditional branching occurs when a program branches to a new location in the code without analyzing data and making a decision. An unconditional branch occurs every time your program encounters the branching instruction. Conditional branching occurs when the program branches based on a decision of some type. This type of branching may or may not occur based on the results of the decision.

The *if* Statement

(It's simply a matter of choice)

Most conditional branching occurs when the program executes an `if` statement, which compares data and decides what to do next based on the result of the comparison. For example, you've probably seen programs that print menus on-screen. To select a menu item, you often type its selection number. When the program receives your input, it checks the number you entered and decides what to do. Listing 6.1 displays a program that illustrates how this type of menu selection might work.

Listing 6.1. MENU1.C is a simple menu program

```c
#include <stdio.h>

int main()
{
    int choice;
```

```
printf("    MENU\n");
printf("------------\n");
printf(" 1. Red\n");
printf(" 2. Green\n");
printf(" 3. Blue\n\n");
printf("Your selection: ");
```

These statements print
a menu on-screen

```
scanf("%d", &choice);

printf("\n");

if (choice == 1)
    printf("You chose red.\n");

if (choice == 2)
    printf("You chose green.\n");

if (choice == 3)
    printf("You chose blue.\n");

return 0;

}
```

The **if** statements determine
the selected menu item

**IN SIMPLE
TERMS**

The program in Listing 6.1 starts by displaying a menu. Using a **scanf()** function, the program asks the user to enter a menu selection that is then stored in the numerical variable **choice**. The last three lines of the program check the value of **choice** and print an appropriate message if the user entered a valid menu selection.

The output of Listing 6.1 is as follows:

```
c:\crook>menu1
    MENU
- - - - - - - - - - - -
 1. Red
 2. Green
 3. Blue

Your selection: 3

You chose blue.

c:\crook>
```

The preceding program prints a menu and lets you enter a menu selection. The program then uses a series of `if` statements to compare the value you entered with the acceptable menu choices. See the pair of equal signs (`==`) in the `if` statements? These are not assignment operators; they are *relational operators* that enable the program to compare two or more values. Look at the first `if` statement in the program. If this line were written in English, it would read "If the value of the variable `choice` equals 1, then print. . . .You chose Red." The other `if` statements in the program have similar meanings.

BUZZWORD

Relational Operators

Relational operators such as the double equal sign (==) enable the program to compare two pieces of data. By comparing variables to constants, for example, you can check variables for specific values. The most common relational operator is the double equal sign, which checks whether two expressions are equal. However, there are also relational operators for such relationships as less than, greater than, and not equal. (You'll see these operators later in this chapter.)

A simple `if` statement includes the keyword `if` followed by a *boolean expression*—an expression that evaluates to either true or false. These are surrounded by parentheses. You follow the parentheses with the statement that you want executed if the boolean expression is true.

The C language is not particular on how you specify the statement to be executed. For example, the statement

```
if (choice == 1)
    printf("You chose red.\n");
```

could also be entered like this:

```
if (choice == 1) printf("You chose red.\n");
```

In other words, although the parantheses are required around the boolean expression, the code to be executed can be on the same line or the following line after the `if` statement.

PLAY BALL!

BUZZWORD

Boolean Expression

A *boolean expression* is an expression that evaluates to either true or false. For example, the expression **3+4=7** is true, whereas the expression **6+1=9** is false. A boolean expression usually compares a variable to a constant or to another variable, such as **num+1=7** or **num1-10=num2**.

How do `if` statements work? Let's say that when you execute the program in Listing 6.1, you type the value 1. When the program gets to the first `if` statement, it checks the value of `choice`. If `choice` equals 1 (which it does, in this case), the program prints the message You chose red and then drops down to the next `if` statement. This time, the program compares the value of `choice` with the number 2. Because `choice` doesn't equal 2, the program ignores the following part of the statement

and drops down to the next `if` statement. The variable `choice` doesn't equal 3 either, so the code portion of the third `if` statement is also ignored. The program ends at this point because there are no more program lines left.

Suppose you enter the number 2 at the menu. When the program gets to the first `if` statement, it discovers that `choice` is not equal to 1, so it ignores the `printf()` of the statement and drops down to the next program line, which is the second `if` statement. Again, the program checks the value of `choice`. Because `choice` equals 2, the program can execute the second portion of the statement; the message `You chose green` is printed on-screen. Program execution drops down to the third `if` statement, which does nothing because `choice` doesn't equal 3.

NOTE

The `if` statement, no matter how complex it becomes, always evaluates to either true or false. If the statement evaluates to true, the second portion of the statement is executed. If the statement evaluates to false, the second portion of the statement is not executed. True and false are actual values: true equals **1**, and false equals **0**. Consequently, the statement **if (1) printf("True!")** tests the value of **1**. Because it evaluates to true, the code prints the message **True!**; but the statement `if` **(0) printf("False!")** evaluates **0** to mean false and therefore does nothing.

Multiline *if* Statements

(Lots of choices)

Listing 6.1 demonstrates the simplest `if` statement. This simple statement usually fits your program's decision-making needs just fine.

Sometimes, however, you want to perform more than one command as part of an if statement. To perform more than one command, enclose the commands within curly braces. Listing 6.2 is a revised version of the menu program that uses this technique.

Listing 6.2. MENU2.C is a new version of the menu program

```c
#include <stdio.h>

int main()
{
    int choice;

    printf("    MENU\n");
    printf("------------\n");
    printf(" 1. Red\n");
    printf(" 2. Green\n");
    printf(" 3. Blue\n\n");
    printf("Your selection: ");

    scanf("%d", &choice);

    printf("\n");

    if (choice == 1)
    {
        printf("\7");
        printf("You chose red.\n");
    }

    if (choice == 2)
    {
        printf("\7\7");
        printf("You chose green.\n");
    }
```

Curly braces are used to enclose multiple lines within an **if** statment

This causes a beep to sound on your computer

continues

C FOR ROOKIES

> **Listing 6.2. Continued**

```c
    if (choice == 3)
    {
        printf("\7\7\7");
        printf("You chose blue.\n");
    }

    return 0;

}
```

IN SIMPLE TERMS

Listing 6.2 is similar to Listing 6.1. The primary difference is that the program makes the speaker of your computer beep before displaying a message. The program prints the menu and then requests the user's menu selection. Next, the three **if** statements compare the user's selection with the possible menu choices. When an **if** statement evaluates to true, the program lines between the curly braces (which beep the speaker and print the message) are executed. Only one **if** statement can possibly evaluate to true, so no more than one message can ever be printed. The sound produced by each menu item sounds for a different number of times.

The output for the program in Listing 6.2 looks like this:

```
c:\crook>menu2
    MENU
- - - - - - - - - - - -
  1. Red
  2. Green
  3. Blue
```

```
Your selection: 1

You chose red.

c:\crook>
```

TIP

Notice that some program lines in Listing 6.2 are indented. By indenting the lines that go with each **if** block, you can more easily see the structure of your program. Listing 6.2 also uses blank lines to separate blocks of code that go together. The compiler doesn't care about the indenting or the blank lines, but these features make your programs easier for you, or another programmer, to read.

What's happening in Listing 6.2? Suppose you run the program and enter the number 2. When the program gets to the first if statement, it compares the value of choice with the number 1. Because these values don't match (or, as programmers say, the statement doesn't evaluate to true), the program skips over every line until it finds the next if statement.

This brings the program to the second if statement. When the program evaluates the expression, it finds that choice equals 2, and it executes the second portion of the if statement. This time the second portion of the statement is not just one command, but two. The program makes the speaker beep and then prints the message.

This brings the program to the last if statement, which the program skips over because choice doesn't equal 3.

CHAPTER 6

NOTE

When you want to set up a multiline **if** statement that executes multiple lines of code, you must use the curly braces—**{** and **}**—to denote the block of instructions that should be executed.

You might think it's a waste of time for the program to evaluate other `if` statements after it finds a match for the menu item you chose. You'd be right, too. When you write programs, you should always look for ways to make them run faster; one way to make a program run faster is to avoid all unnecessary processing. But how, you may ask, do you avoid unnecessary processing when you have to compare a variable with more than one value?

One way to keep processing to a minimum is to use C's `else` statement. This keyword enables you to use a single `if` statement to choose between two outcomes. When the `if` statement evaluates to true, the second part of the statement is executed. When the `if` statement evaluates to false, the `else` portion is executed. When the `if` statement evaluates to neither true nor false, it's time to get a new computer. Listing 6.3 demonstrates how `else` works.

Listing 6.3. HELLO1.C recognizes the name of its user

```c
#include <stdio.h>

int main()
{
    char name[100];

    printf("Please enter your name: ");
    scanf("%s", &name);

    if (strcmp(name, "Fred") == 0)          Used to compare
        printf("Hi, Fred!\n");              a string
```

```
else ─────────────────────────────
    printf("Hello, stranger.\n");

return 0;
}
```

*The **else** statement enables **if** statements to handle two outcomes*

IN SIMPLE TERMS

Listing 6.3 asks the user for his name. If the user types **Fred**, the program prints the message **Hi, Fred!**. Then, skipping over the **else** clause, the program drops down to the **return 0** statement, which ends the program. If the user types something other than **Fred**, the program skips to the **else** statement and instead prints the message **Hello, stranger**.

Here is the output for Listing 6.3:

```
c:\crook>hello1
Please enter your name: Fred
Hi, Fred!

c:\crook>
```

When you run this program, you're asked to enter your name. If you enter the name **Fred**, the program recognizes you and gives you a personal hello. Otherwise, the program considers you a stranger and treats you accordingly. (If you like, you can personalize the program by changing all occurrences of **Fred** to your name.) As you can see, the else clause is executed only when the if statement is false. If the if statement is true, the program ignores the else clause.

The program in Listing 6.3 also demonstrates how to compare strings. Strings are compared with the strcmp() function. You will compare strings often in your programs, especially programs that require text input from the user. By using string comparisons, you can catch an incorrect response to a prompt and print an error message on-screen to inform the user of the incorrect entry.

CAUTION

Two strings can only be compared with the **strcmp()** function. At first glance, it would appear to be possible to use the **==** operator to compare two strings. However the C language does not allow strings to be compared with the **==** operator. You must use the **strcmp()** function anytime two strings are to be compared.

The `else` statement provides a default outcome for an `if` statement. A default outcome doesn't help much, however, in an `if` statement that has to deal with more than two possible outcomes (as in the previous menu program). Suppose you want Listing 6.3 to recognize your friends' names too. No problem. First, get some friends; then use the second form of the `else` keyword, as shown in Listing 6.4.

Listing 6.4. HELLO2.C recognizes three different users

```c
#include <stdio.h>

int main()
{
   char name[100];

   printf("Please enter your name: ");
   scanf("%s", &name);

   if (strcmp(name, "Fred") == 0)
      printf("Hi, Fred!\n");
   else if (strcmp(name, "Sarah") == 0)
      printf("How's it going, Sarah?\n");
   else if (strcmp(name, "Tony") == 0)
      printf("Hey! It's my man Tony!\n");
   else
      printf("Hello, stranger.\n");

   return 0;
}
```

The **else** statement allows **if** statements to handle many outcomes

IN SIMPLE TERMS

Listing 6.4 asks for the user's name. Next, the **if** statement checks for the name **Fred**. If the user entered **Fred**, the program prints Fred's message. Otherwise, the **else** statement checks for other names and prints an appropriate message if a match is found. If none of the names match the user's input, the final **else** clause executes and prints a generic message on-screen.

The output for Listing 6.4 looks like this:

```
c:\crook>hello2
Please enter your name: Sarah
How's it going, Sarah?

c:\crook>
```

In Listing 6.4, as in Listing 6.3, you're asked to enter a name. But this time, the program uses an `if` statement with a series of `else` clauses that contain additional `if` statements to check the name entered against the names the program can recognize. When the program finds a match, it skips over any remaining `else` statements. If the program finds no match—that is, the user hasn't entered the name **Fred**, **Sarah**, or **Tony**—the `else` clause executes and provides a default response. This default ensures that no matter what the user types, he or she will receive a greeting. This greeting may save you a great deal of grief and money; disgruntled computer users are famous for punching monitor screens and throwing keyboards.

Listing 6.5 is a new version of the menu program that uses the `else` statement. You should now know enough about computer decision-making to figure out how it works.

C FOR ROOKIES

> **Listing 6.5. MENU3.C runs more efficiently than previous versions of the program**

```c
#include <stdio.h>

int main()
{
   int choice;

   printf("    MENU\n");
   printf("------------\n");
   printf(" 1. Red\n");
   printf(" 2. Green\n");
   printf(" 3. Blue\n\n");
   printf("Your selection: ");

   scanf("%d", &choice);

   printf("\n");

   if (choice == 1)
   {
      printf("\7");
      printf("You chose red.\n");
   }
   else if (choice == 2)
   {
      printf("\7\7");
      printf("You chose green.\n");
   }
   else if (choice == 3)
   {
      printf("\7\7\7");
      printf("You chose blue.\n");
   }
   else
   {
      printf("Invalid selection!\n");
   }
```

A series of **else** statements is faster than using many **if** statements

120

```
    return 0;

}
```

**IN SIMPLE
TERMS**

Listing 6.5 prints a menu, then asks the user to enter a menu selection. The **if** statement compares the user's input with the acceptable menu values. If it finds a match, the program sounds the computer's speaker and prints a message. If it finds no match, the program displays an error message and ends.

Here's the output for Listing 6.5:

```
c:\crook>menu3
     MENU
------------
 1. Red
 2. Green
 3. Blue

Your selection: 2

You chose green.

c:\crook>
```

Relational Operators

(How do you compare?)

The previous programs in this chapter used only the equal operator to compare values. Often you'll need to compare values in other ways.

C FOR ROOKIES

You might, for example, want to know if a value is less than or greater than another value. The C language features an entire set of relational operators you can use in `if` statements and other types of comparisons. These operators include not only the double equal sign (==), but also not equal to (!=), less than (<), greater than(>), less than or equal (<=), and greater than or equal (>=). These operators are summarized in Table 6.1.

Table 6.1. Relational operators

Operator	Meaning	Examples
==	Equals	3==(4-1)
!=	Not equal	5!=(3+3)
<	Less than	3<23
>	Greater than	41>39
<=	Less than or equal	5<=6
>=	Greater than or equal	10>=10

Listing 6.6 demonstrates the use of the (<) operator.

Listing 6.6. NUMRNGE1.C determines the size of a number

```
#include <stdio.h>

int main()
{
   int number;

   printf("Enter a number no larger than 50: ");
   scanf("%d", &number);

   if (number < 10)
      printf("Your number is less than 10.\n");
   else if (number < 20)
      printf("Your number is greater than 9 and less than
             20.\n");
```

Relational operators let you check for many types of relationships between data

```
else if (number < 30)
    printf("Your number is greater than 19 and less than
            30.\n");
else if (number < 40)
    printf("Your number is greater than 29 and less than
            40.\n");
else if (number < 50)
    printf("Your number is greater than 39 and less than
            50.\n");
else if (number == 50)
    printf("Your number is 50.\n");
else
    printf("Your number is out of the acceptable range.\n");

    return 0;
}
```

IN SIMPLE TERMS

Listing 6.6 asks the user to enter a number no greater than 50. After the user types the number, the program uses an **if** statement with a series of **else** clauses to determine the range within which the number falls. For this determination, the program uses the less-than operator (**<**). If the selected number is less than the numerical constant in the **if** statement or **else** clause, the program prints an appropriate message to the user. If the number is larger than the constant, the program moves on to the next clause and again makes the comparison, this time with a higher numerical constant. Finally, if the number turns out to be larger than the allowed maximum of 50, the program prints an error message.

The output for Listing 6.6 looks like this:

```
c:\crook>numrnge1
Enter a number no larger than 50: 60
Your number is out of the acceptable range.

c:\crook>
```

When you run the program shown in Listing 6.6, the program asks that you enter a number no larger than 50. After you type the number, the program determines the number's range and prints a message informing you of this range. This program doesn't just demonstrate the use of the (<) operator; it keeps you off the streets by making you do a lot of typing. More important, Listing 6.6 further illustrates the way a block of if and else statements work.

Suppose when you run the program in Listing 6.6, you type the number **9**. When the program gets to the first if statement, it compares 9 to 10 and discovers that 9 is less than 10. (And to think you paid hundreds of dollars for a machine to tell you that.) The if statement then evaluates to true and the program prints the following message:

```
Your number is less than 10.
```

Look at the block of else statements that go along with the if statement. Isn't 9 also less than 20? Moreover, isn't 9 also less than 30, 40, and 50? Why don't you see the messages associated with all of these else statements, as well as the message associated with the if? And why, when you drop a piece of buttered bread, does it always land butter-side down? (Just thought I'd ask.)

The answer to the first question has to do with the way the if–else block works. (The answer to the second question will never be known, so we'll just ignore it.) When an if or else evaluates to true, the program skips the rest of the statements in the block—or, as programmers say, the program branches to the next statement after the block. In the case of Listing 6.6, there is no statement after the block, so the program simply ends.

Logical Operators

(Your computer as Spock)

A single comparison in an `if` statement often isn't enough to determine whether data matches your criteria. How can you be sure, for example, that the user enters a number within a specific range? You could hold a gun to the user's head as he's typing the data. Although this may ensure that data is entered properly, it requires that you stay by the computer at all times. Hardly practical. A better way to ensure that data is in the correct range is to use logical operators in your `if` statements.

Let's say that the user is asked to enter a number between 10 and 50, inclusive. To discover whether a number is within this range, you must check not only that the number is greater than or equal to 10, but also that the number is less than or equal to 50. To help handle these situations, C features three logical operators—AND, OR, and NOT—that can be used to combine expressions in an `if` statement. A *logical operator* works on variables to return a result based on the value of the variables in conjunction with a rational condition.

PLAY BALL!

BUZZWORD

Logical Operators

Logical operators, including **&&** *(AND),* **¦¦** *(OR), and* **!** *(NOT), enable you to evaluate more than one condition in a single* **if** *statement.*

The AND (`&&`) operator requires all expressions to be true for the entire expression to be true. For example, the expression `(3+2=5)` `&&` `(6+2=8)` is true because the expressions on both sides of the `&&` are true. However, the expression `(4+3=9)` `&&` `(3+3=6)` is not true because the expression on the left of the `&&` is not true. Remember this when combining expressions with AND: If any expression is false, the entire expression is false.

The OR operator (¦¦) requires only one expression to be true for the entire expression to be true. For example, the expressions (3+6=2) ¦¦ (4+4=8) and (4+1=5) ¦¦ (7+2=9) are both true because at least one of the expressions being compared is true. Notice that in the second case both expressions being compared are true, which also makes an OR expression true.

The NOT (!) operator switches the value of (or negates) a logical expression. For example, the expression (4+3=5) is not true; however, the expression !(4+3=5) is true. Take a look at the following expression:

```
(4+5=9) && !(3+1=3)
```

Is this expression true or false? If you said true, you understand the way the logical operators work. The expressions on either side of the && are both true, so the entire expression is true. If you said false, you must go to bed without any dinner.

Of course, you wouldn't write expressions like (4+5=9) && !(3+1=3) in your programs. They would serve no purpose because you already know how the expressions evaluate. However, when you use variables, you have no way of knowing in advance how an expression may evaluate. For example, is the expression (num < 9) && (num > 15) true or false? You don't know without being told the value of the numerical variable num. By using logical operators in your if statement, though, your program can do the evaluation, and, based on the result—true or false—take the appropriate action.

Listing 6.7 demonstrates how logical operators work. When you run the program, it asks you to enter a number between 10 and 50. If you type a number out of that range, the program lets you know. Although Listing 6.7 is similar to Listing 6.6, it works very differently. After the user types a number, the program uses a single if statement to determine whether the number is within the acceptable range. If the number is out of range, the program prints an error message and ends.

Listing 6.7. NUMRNGE2.C stops the program when it discovers improper input

```c
#include <stdio.h>

int main()
{
    int number;

    printf("Enter a number between 10 and 50: ");
    scanf("%d", &number);

    if (number < 10 || number > 50)
        printf("The number %d is out of range!\n", number);
    else
        printf("The number %d is in range.\n", number);

    return 0;

}
```

Logical operators permit many comparisons with a single **if** statement

IN SIMPLE TERMS

Listing 6.7 asks the user to enter a number between 10 and 50. The program then compares the number entered with the constants 10 and 50. If the number is less than 10 or greater than 50, the program prints an error message and ends. Otherwise, program execution branches to the next **else** statement, which results in a different message being printed on-screen.

The output for Listing 6.7 looks like this:

```
c:\crook>numrnge2
Enter a number between 10 and 50: 35
The number 35 is in range.

c:\crook>
```

127

The Infamous *GOTO*

(Using Unconditional Branching)

Most of this chapter has been dedicated to conditional branches. If you recall, however, programmers can also use unconditional branches. This type of branching can be accomplished by using the goto instruction, which forces program execution to branch to a specific label.

Listing 6.8 is a C program that uses the goto instruction to branch to a specific place in the program. The destination of the branch is marked by the label lessthan.

Listing 6.8. GOTOEX.C demonstrates the *goto* command

```
#include <stdio.h>

int main()
{
   int number;

   printf("Please enter a number: ");
   scanf("%d", &number);

   if (number <= 100)
      goto lessthan;

   printf("Your number is greater than 100.\n");
   return 0;

   lessthan:

      printf("Your number is less than or equal to 100.\n");

   return 0;

}
```

The **goto** statement is rarely used in C programs

CHAPTER 6

C FOR ROOKIES

**IN SIMPLE
TERMS**

Listing 6.8 uses the **scanf()** function to get a number from
the user. Next, the **if** statement checks whether the number
is less than or equal to 100. If it is, the **goto** statement is
executed. The **goto** statement sends program execution to
the label **lessthan**, at which point the program prints an
appropriate message and ends. If the number the user enters
is greater than 100, the **if** statement evaluates to false. In
this case, program execution drops down to the next line, the
program prints a message, and the **return 0** statement ends
the program.

Here is the output for Listing 6.8:

```
c:\crook>gotoex
Please enter a number: 132
Your number is greater than 100.

c:\crook>
```

In Listing 6.8, notice that when the label's name follows the goto, it
doesn't include a colon; however, the actual point in the program where
the label is declared does include a colon. Notice also that this program
uses the command return 0 to stop the program's execution. Although
you have only seen it at the very end of programs, it can be used in other
locations to allow the program to terminate early. The above program
includes the statement return 0 halfway through the program. This
gives the programmer more flexibility in deciding when the program
should terminate.

NOTE

Although the **goto** statement may seem like a handy thing to
have around, it has been so misused in the past that most

continues

129

C FOR ROOKIES

continued

programmers avoid it like nuclear waste. Use of **goto** can turn a program into a tangled, unreadable mess. A modern, structured language like C has no need for the **goto** instruction. It is included in C only to keep the language compatible with earlier programming languages. This is the first and last time you will see the **goto** instruction in this book. Always try to avoid using it in your programs. Start developing good programming habits now and *never use* **goto** in your programs. (Get the hint?)

As soon as you understand all this stuff about computer decision-making, you'll be close to becoming a C programmer. Making decisions is, after all, one of the most important things a program does. It's safe to say that there's not a single worthwhile program on the planet that doesn't use `if` statements or something similar.

Common Rookie Mistakes

Backward logic. Often, an `if` statement containing several expressions joined by logical operators is confusing. It is sometimes necessary to add parentheses not only to organize the expressions, but also to be sure that the expressions are evaluated in the proper order. Remember that expressions are evaluated from the inner-most set of parenthesis out. For example:

```
if ((num > 10) && (num < 20)) ¦¦ (!choice)
    ...
```

Unexpected values in input. Remember that when you use the scanf() function, the user can type virtually anything. It's up to your program to ensure that the value entered is appropriate for the program. For this reason, adding an else clause to an if statement is a good idea. It ensures that every possible value gets a response from the program.

Confusing the less-than and greater-than operators. Because the less-than operator (<) and the greater-than operator (>) look so much alike, it's easy to get them confused. Here's a trick to help you learn which is which: The small side of the operator (the point) always points to the smaller value and the large side of the operator always points to the larger value.

Overusing goto. There's no need to use goto in your programs. This book included a brief discussion on goto only because you may see it in other programs and you need to know how it works.

Comparing strings with the == operator. Strings can only be compared using the strcmp() function. They cannot be compared with the == operator.

Summing Up

▼ Program flow is the order in which a program executes its statements.

▼ When a computer program branches, it jumps to a new location in the code and continues execution from there.

▼ An if statement compares the values of data and decides what statements to execute based on that evaluation.

▼ The `else` statement allows `if` statements to handle many different outcomes.

▼ The relational operators—equals (`==`), does not equal (`!=`), less than (`<`), greater than (`>`), less than or equal (`<=`), and greater than or equal (`>=`)—enable programs to compare data in various ways.

▼ Logical operators—AND (`&&`), OR (`¦¦`), and NOT (`!`)—enable an `if` statement to evaluate more than one expression, yet they still resolve the expressions to a single true or false.

In the next chapter, you'll learn about looping constructs, which allow your programs to perform repetitive tasks—another thing that computers are extraordinarily good at.

CHAPTER 7

Repetitive Operations

(Over and Over and Over and...)

IN A NUTSHELL

▼ Understanding program looping
▼ Using **for, while,** and **do–while** loops
▼ Knowing when to use each type of loop

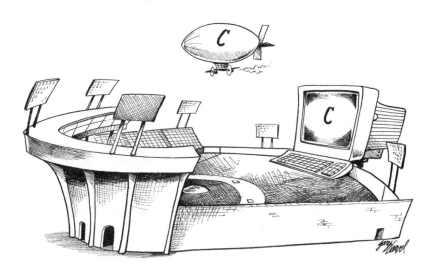

C FOR ROOKIES

A computer handles repetitive operations especially well—it never gets bored, and it can perform a task as well the 10,000th time as it did the first. Consider, for example, a disk file containing 10,000 names and addresses. If you tried to type labels for all those people, you'd be seeing spots before your eyes in no time. On the other hand, a printer (with the aid of a computer) can tirelessly spit out all 10,000 labels—and with nary a complaint to the union.

Every language must have some form of looping command to instruct a computer to perform repetitive tasks. C features three types of looping: `for` loops, `while` loops, and `do–while` loops. In this chapter, you learn to use these powerful statements.

BUZZWORD

Looping

In computer programs, *looping* is the process of repeatedly running a block of statements. Starting at the top of the block, the statements are executed until the program reaches the end of the block, at which point the program goes back to the top and starts over. The statements in the block may be repeated any number of times, from once to forever. If a loop continues on forever, it is called an *infinite loop*.

The *for* Loop

(Around and around we go)

Probably the most often used loop in C is the `for` loop, which instructs a program to perform a block of code a specified number of times. You could, for example, use a `for` loop to instruct your computer to print those 10,000 address labels. Because you don't currently have an address

file, however, let's say you want to print your name on-screen six times. Listing 7.1 shows one way to do this.

Listing 7.1. REPEAT.C prints your name six times

```c
#include <stdio.h>

int main()
{
    char name[255];

    printf("Please enter your name: ");
    scanf("%s", &name);

    printf("%s\n", name);
    printf("%s\n", name);
    printf("%s\n", name);
    printf("%s\n", name);
    printf("%s\n", name);
    printf("%s\n", name);

    return 0;
}
```

Anywhere with repeated commands may be a good place for a loop

The program output for Listing 7.1 looks like this:

```
c:\crook>repeat
Please enter your name: Shawn
Shawn
Shawn
Shawn
Shawn
Shawn
Shawn

c:\crook>
```

C FOR ROOKIES

IN SIMPLE TERMS

Listing 7.1 uses the **scanf()** function to request the user's name. A series of **printf()** statements then prints the name on-screen six times.

Look at Listing 7.1. See all those `printf()` statements? As a computer programmer, whenever you see program code containing many identical instructions, a little bell should go off in your head. When you hear this little bell, you should do one of two things:

1. Answer your telephone.

2. Say to yourself, "Hmmmm. This looks like a good place for a loop."

Having many lines in your program containing identical instructions makes your program longer than necessary and wastes valuable memory. It also shows poor programming style. Unless you want your programming friends to snicker behind your back, learn to replace redundant program code with program loops.

TIP

To produce programs that are tightly written, shorter, and faster, always try to replace repetitive program code with program loops.

Listing 7.1 can be streamlined easily by using a `for` loop, and Listing 7.2 shows how. The output of the second version is identical to the first (except a different name was entered); now the program is shorter and contains no redundant code.

Listing 7.2. LOOP1.C prints your name six times using a *for* loop

```c
#include <stdio.h>

int main()
{
   char name[255];
   int x;

   printf("Please enter your name: ");
   scanf("%s", &name);

   for (x=1; x<=6; x=x+1)
      printf("%s\n", name);

   return 0;
}
```

for (x=1; x<=6; x=x+1) ——— Repeated commands replaced by a **for** loop

IN SIMPLE TERMS

Listing 7.2 requests the user's name with the **scanf()** function. The user's name is then printed on-screen six times within a **for** loop.

The output for Listing 7.2 looks like this:

```
c:\crook>loop1
Please enter your name: Justin
Justin
Justin
Justin
Justin
Justin
Justin

c:\crook>
```

137

Look at the program line beginning with the keyword `for`. The loop starts with this line. The word `for` tells C that you're starting a `for` loop. Look at the line again:

```
for (x=1; x<=6; x=x+1)
```

There are actually three elements inside the parentheses. The first part, `x=1`, is called the initialization section. The second part, `x<=6`, is called the condition; the last part, `x=x+1`, is called the increment.

All three sections of the `for` loop make reference to the *loop-control variable* x. The loop-control variable, which can have any integer-variable name, is where C stores the current loop count. Notice that the loop-control variable must have been previously declared as an `int` (integer) variable.

PLAY BALL!

BUZZWORD

Loop-Control Variable

A *loop-control variable* holds the current loop count. When the value of this variable reaches the requested loop count, the loop ends.

The initialization section of the `for` statement is used to initialize the loop-control variable that controls the action. The condition section represents a boolean condition that should be equal to true for the loop to continue execution. Finally, the increment, which is the third part of the statement, is a statement describing how to increment the index variable. The statement after the `for` statement, in this case `printf("%s\n", name)`, is executed each time the `for` loop is found to be true.

IN SIMPLE TERMS

In Listing 7.2, when the **for** loop begins, C places the number 1 in the variable **x**. The program then drops down to the next line, which prints the user's name. The statement **x=x+1** tells C to increment (increase by one) the loop-control variable and execute the loop again. So, **x** becomes **2**, and the program executes the **printf()** line. The program then evaluates the statement **x<=6** to see if it is true. If the loop count (in **x**) is less than or equal to the number **6**, the program executes the loop again. This process continues until **x** is greater than **6**.

Whew! Got all that? Or did you fall asleep halfway through? If you just woke up, rub the fuzzies from your eyes and read the Simple Terms box a couple times to make sure it sinks in. If you still can't stay awake, take a nap.

BUZZWORD

PLAY BALL!

Increment/Decrement

In computer programs, variables are often incremented and decremented. When you *increment* a variable, you add some value to it. When you *decrement* a variable, you subtract some value from it. If the value of the increment or decrement is not explicit, it's assumed that the value is 1. For example, the statement "The program increments the variable **num** by 5" means that **num** is increased in value by 5. On the other hand, the statement "The program increments **num**" means that **num** is increased by 1.

Suppose you want to modify Listing 7.2 to print your name 10 times. What would you change? If you answered, "I'd change the 6 in the **for**

line to 10," you win the Programmer of the Week award. If you answered, "I'd change my socks," you must go directly to jail. Do not pass Go, do not collect $200.

Changing the Increment Value

(Watch your step on this ride)

The previous example of a `for` loop increments the loop counter by 1. But suppose you want a `for` loop that counts from 5 to 50 by fives? This could be useful if you need to use the loop counter to display a value that needs to be incremented by a different number. You can do this by changing the increment section of a `for` loop, as shown in Listing 7.3.

Listing 7.3. LOOP2.C changes the increment value in a *for* loop

```
#include <stdio.h>

int main()
{
    char name[255];
    int x;

    printf("Please enter your name: ");
    scanf("%s", &name);

    for (x=5; x<=50; x=x+5)
    {
        printf("%s\n", name);
        printf("Loop counter value: %d\n", x);
    }

    return 0;
}
```

This loop counts from 5 to 50 in increments of 5

*Multiple lines can be the focus of a **for** loop by using curly braces*

IN SIMPLE TERMS

Listing 7.3 uses the **scanf()** function to get the user's name. The program then executes a **for** loop that prints the user's name and the current value of the loop-control variable 10 times. Because the **for** loop contains the increment statement **x=x+5**, 5 is added to the control variable each time through the loop.

The output of Listing 7.3 looks like this:

```
c:\crook>loop2
Please enter your name: John
John
Loop counter value: 5
John
Loop counter value: 10
John
Loop counter value: 15
John
Loop counter value: 20
John
Loop counter value: 25
John
Loop counter value: 30
John
Loop counter value: 35
John
Loop counter value: 40
John
Loop counter value: 45
John
Loop counter value: 50

c:\crook>
```

When you run this program, you're asked to enter your name. The program then prints both your name and the current value of the loop variable 10 times. Besides showing how to use the increment part of a `for` loop, this program also shows how you can place more than one command in the body of a `for` loop. You surround the statements to be executed inside curly braces (`{` and `}`). You can, in fact, have as many statements as you want between the curly braces. Remember that they all will be executed each time through the loop.

PLAY BALL!

BUZZWORD

Body of a Loop

The *body of a loop* comprises the commands that are performed each time through the loop. In a **for** loop, this is the statement directly after the **for** statement, or any group of statements inside curly braces.

Look closely at the `for` loop in Listing 7.3. Unlike the previous programs, this loop doesn't start counting at 1. Rather, the loop variable begins with a value of 5. Then, thanks to the `x=x+5` statement, the loop variable is incremented by 5 each time through the loop. Therefore, `x` goes from 5 to 10, from 10 to 15, and so on up to 50, resulting in 10 loops.

Listing 7.4 shows how you can use the `increment` value to count backward. (Well, it won't help *you* count backward, but it'll help your computer.) Notice that the condition part of the `for` statement is in reverse order; that is, the higher value comes first. Notice also that the increment clause uses a negative value, which causes the loop count to be decremented (decreased) rather than incremented. Finally, notice that no matter how hard you try, you can't whistle "The Star Spangled Banner" out of your right ear. This has little to do with computing, but it is nevertheless one of the great mysteries of the cosmos.

Listing 7.4. LOOP3.C uses the increment clause in a *for* loop to count backward

```c
#include <stdio.h>

int main()
{
   char name[255];
   int x;

   printf("Please enter your name: ");
   scanf("%s", &name);

   for (x=50; x>=5; x=x-5)
   {
      printf("%s\n", name);
      printf("Loop counter value: %d\n", x);
   }

   return 0;
}
```

This loop counts backward by five

IN SIMPLE TERMS

Listing 7.4 uses the **scanf()** function to get the user's name. The program then executes a **for** statement, which prints the user's name and the current value of the loop variable 10 times. Because the **for** loop contains the clause **x=x-5**, 5 is subtracted from the control variable each time through the loop. The **for** loop also uses the statement **x=50** to initialize the starting value of **x** to **50**, and then checks to make sure **x** is greater than or equal to 5 with the statement **x>=5**.

The output for Listing 7.4 looks like this:

```
c:\crook>loop3
Please enter your name: Harry
Harry
Loop counter value: 50
Harry
Loop counter value: 45
Harry
Loop counter value: 40
Harry
Loop counter value: 35
Harry
Loop counter value: 30
Harry
Loop counter value: 25
Harry
Loop counter value: 20
Harry
Loop counter value: 15
Harry
Loop counter value: 10
Harry
Loop counter value: 5

c:\crook>
```

The Increment and Decrement Operators

(Incrementing and decrementing operators the easy way)

Every for loop increments or decrements the control variable in some way. For example:

```
for (x=0; x<50; x=x+1)
    ...;
```

As you know, the part of the above statement that increments the control variable is x=x+1.

The C language actually has two operators that are a short-cut to incrementing or decrementing a variable. One of these operators is called the increment operator (++), the other is called the decrement operator (−−).

To increment a variable by one, use the statement:

```
x++;
```

The above statement has the same result as if you had typed x=x+1. To decrement a variable by one, use the statement:

```
x--;
```

This statement has exactly the same result as if you had typed x=x-1. The increment and decrement operators can be used alone (as above), or inside a for loop. For example, the statement:

```
for (x=0; x<50; x++)
    ...;
```

does exactly the same thing as the previous for loop, and that is increment the variable x by one.

C programmers prefer using the ++ or −− operator because it is a more compact method of changing the value of a variable. Not only is x++ or x−− easier to read (once you know what it means) than x=x+1 or x=x-1, it is also faster to type!

There is one limitation with using the increment or decrement operator and that is the variable that is being operated on can only be incremented or decremented by one. If you have a variable that must be incremented by a larger value, you must resort to x=x+2 or x=x+5.

CHAPTER 7

However, most `for` loops always increment a variable by one, therefore you will see the increment and decrement operator used extensively in C.

Using Variables in Loops

(Where we'll stop, nobody knows)

Just as you can substitute most numerical values in a program, you can also substitute variables for the constants in a `for` loop. In fact, you'll probably use variables in your loop limits as often as you use constants, if not more. Listing 7.5 shows how to do this.

Listing 7.5. LOOP4.C uses a variable for one of the loop limits

```c
#include <stdio.h>

int main()
{
   char name[255];
   int x;
   int count;

   printf("Please enter your name: ");
   scanf("%s", &name);
   printf("Please enter the print count: ");
   scanf("%d", &count);

   printf("\n");

   for (x=1; x<=count; x++)
   {
```

A variable makes this loop more versatile

146

```
        printf("%s\n", name);
        printf("Loop counter value: %d\n", x);
    }

    return 0;
}
```

IN SIMPLE TERMS

Listing 7.5 uses two **scanf()** functions to get the user's name and the number of times the user wants his name printed. The program then prints a blank line, after which it initiates a **for** loop that prints the user's name and the current value of the loop-control variable **count** times.

The output for Listing 7.5 looks like this:

```
c:\crook>loop4
Please enter your name: Tom
Please enter the print count: 7

Tom
Loop counter value: 1
Tom
Loop counter value: 2
Tom
Loop counter value: 3
Tom
Loop counter value: 4
Tom
Loop counter value: 5
Tom
Loop counter value: 6
Tom
Loop counter value: 7

c:\crook>
```

When you run this program, you're asked to enter your name and the number of times you want it printed. The program then prints your name the requested number of times. As you can see in Listing 7.5, you can have the program print your name any number of times because the loop's upper limit is contained in the variable `count`. The `count` variable gets its value from you at the start of each program run.

Using variables in `for` loops makes your programs more flexible and produces a powerful programming statement. As you'll soon see, you can use variables with other types of loops too. In fact, you can use a numerical variable in a program in most places a numerical value is required. You can even use numerical variables in salads, but they taste bitter and leave a yucky film on your tongue.

Using *while* Loops

(Getting dizzy yet?)

Another type of loop you can use in your programs is the while loop. Unlike a for loop, which loops the number of times given in the loop limits, a while loop continues running until its control expression becomes true. The *control expression* is a boolean expression much like the boolean expressions you used with if statements. In other words, any expression that evaluates to true or false can be used as a control expression for a while loop. Listing 7.6 shows a while loop in action.

> **Listing 7.6. LOOP5.C demonstrates a *while* loop**

```
#include <stdio.h>

int main()
{
    int num;
```

```
    num = 1; ———————————————— Initialization of the control variable

    while (num != 0)——————————— Boolean expression
    {
        printf("Please enter a number: ");
        scanf("%d", &num);
    }

    printf("Looping is finished.\n");

    return 0;
}
```

**IN SIMPLE
TERMS**

Listing 7.6 sets the variable **num** to **1**, which allows the
program to enter the **while** loop. The **while** loop contains the
scanf() function that asks the user to enter a number. The
loop repeats until the user enters **0**, after which the program
prints a brief message and ends.

The output for Listing 7.6 looks like this:

```
c:\crook>loop5
Please enter a number: 8
Please enter a number: 2
Please enter a number: 45
Please enter a number: 99
Please enter a number: 123
Please enter a number: 1
Please enter a number: 0
Looping is finished.

c:\crook>
```

Loop-Control Expression

A *loop-control expression* is a boolean expression that determines whether a loop should continue or end. In a **while** loop, when the control expression becomes false, the loop ends. As long as the control expression is true, the loop continues.

How does the `while` loop in Listing 7.6 work? First, the loop variable num is set to 1. Then, at the start of the `while` loop, the program compares the value in num with the constant 0. If these two values don't match, the expression evaluates to false, and the program executes the body of the loop, which in this case is a `printf()` and `scanf()` statement. These statements get a number from the user and store it in the variable num. The program then comes to the end of the curly braces, which tells C that it has reached the end of the loop and must now go back and check the value of num again.

If the user entered a value other than 0, the two values in the loop's control expression again don't match, and the body of the loop (the `printf()` and `scanf()` lines) executes one more time. If the values match, the control expression evaluates to true, the loop ends, and the program branches to the first statement after the curly braces, which in the case of Listing 7.6, is a `printf()` statement.

Notice how the program sets the variable num to 1 before the `while` loop starts. This is important because it ensures that the value in num starts at a value other than 0. If num did happen to start at 0, the program would never get to the body of the `while` loop. Instead, the loop's control expression would immediately evaluate to true, and the program would branch to the statement after the curly braces. Mistakes like this make programmers growl at their loved ones and answer the phone with, "What do you want, idiot?"

CAUTION

Always *initialize* (set the starting value of) any variable used in a **while** loop's control expression. Failure to do so may result in your program skipping over the loop entirely.

Initializing a variable means setting it to its starting value. If you need a variable to start at a specific value, you must initialize it yourself.

The *do-while* Loop

(Nearing the end of the ride)

C also features do–while loops. A do–while loop is much like a while loop, except a do–while loop evaluates its control expression at the end of the loop rather than at the beginning. So the body of the loop—the statements between the beginning and end of the loop—is always executed at least once. In a while loop, the body of the loop may or may not ever get executed. Listing 7.7 shows how a do–while loop works.

Listing 7.7. LOOP6.C demonstrates a *do–while* loop

```
#include <stdio.h>

int main()
{
    int num;

    do
    {
        printf("Please enter a number: ");
        scanf("%d", &num);
    }
```

*A **do–while** loop checks its control expression at the bottom of the loop*

continues

Listing 7.7. Continued

```
    while (num != 0);

    printf("Looping is finished.\n");

    return 0;
}
```

**IN SIMPLE
TERMS**

Listing 7.7 enters a **do–while** loop. In the loop, the user is asked to enter a number. The **scanf()** statement gets the number and repeats until the user enters a value of **0**, after which the program prints a brief message and ends.

The output for Listing 7.7 looks like this:

```
c:\crook>loop6
Please enter a number: 12
Please enter a number: 23
Please enter a number: 1
Please enter a number: 5
Please enter a number: 99
Please enter a number: 0
Looping is finished.

c:\crook>
```

When you run Listing 7.7, you're asked to enter a number. As long as you enter a number other than **0**, the program continues to loop. When you finally enter **0**, the loop ends.

Notice that you don't need to initialize the loop-control variable num before entering the loop. The num variable gets its value from the scanf() statement that comes before the loop's control statement is

initiated. So if people have stopped calling your house because they're tired of being called idiots, try changing your `while` loops to `do–while` loops. The variable `num` always holds a valid value when the program reaches the `while` portion of the loop, where `num` is compared with `0`.

TIP

Different looping methods work best in different programming situations. Although experience is the best teacher, you should keep some things in mind when selecting a looping construct. When you want a loop to run a specific number of times, the **for** loop is usually the best choice. When you want a loop to run until a certain condition is met, the **while** or **do–while** loops work best. Remember that the body of a **do–while** loop is always run at least once because the control expression is checked at the bottom of the loop. A **while** loop, on the other hand, is not guaranteed to execute at all because its control expression is evaluated first—at the top of the loop.

Putting It Together

(One last spin)

You've learned a lot about program looping in this chapter, and you're probably not sure how or why you would use these techniques. Listings 7.8 through 7.10 give you the chance to broaden your experience with the three looping constructs. When you run any of the programs, you're asked to enter a multidigit number that contains the digit 9. After you enter the string, the program uses one of the looping techniques to find and mark the location of the substring **9** from what you entered.

All three programs yield similar program output, but each uses a different looping technique to get the job done. Be sure you understand these programs before you move on to the next chapter. Looping is a valuable tool to use when writing programs. You'll use it more than a cat uses a litter box.

Listing 7.8. LOOPDEM1.C uses a *for* loop to locate a substring

```c
#include <stdio.h>

int main()
{
   char string[255];
   int x;
   int location;

   printf("Enter a string containing the number '9': ");
   scanf("%s", string);

   location = 0;
   for (x=0; x<strlen(string); x++) ———————— This loop finds the digit 9
      if (string[x] == '9')
         location = x;

   if (location==0)
   {
      printf("Number '9' not found.\n");
   }
   else
   {
      printf("Number '9' located.\n");
      printf("%s\n", string);
      for (x=0; x<location; x++)———————— This loop displays the
         printf(" ");                    caret in the appropriate
                                         location
```

```
        printf("^\n");
    }

    return 0;
}
```

IN SIMPLE TERMS

Listing 7.8 asks the user to enter a multidigit number containing the digit **9**. The program then initializes the variable **location**, which holds the location of the substring **9**, to **0**. A **for** loop is then executed. This loop's limit is from **1** to the length of the string that the user entered.

Within the loop, the comparison `if (string[x] == '9')` uses the loop-control variable as the starting location at which to check for the requested substring. By using this variable, the `if` statement moves forward through the string a character at a time, looking for the substring **9**. When the `if` statement evaluates to true, the variable `location` is set to the value of the loop variable `x`. The `for` loop continues until it reaches the end of the string.

If `location` is still **0** when the loop finishes, the substring was not found. The program then prints an error message. If `location` is greater than **0**, the program prints the contents of `string`, which is the string the user entered. The program then uses another `for` loop to print enough spaces to place the cursor immediately beneath the first character of the substring `loop`, at which point it prints a caret marking the substring's location.

> **Listing 7.9. LOOPDEM2.C uses a *while* loop to locate a substring**

```c
#include <stdio.h>

int main()
{
   char string[255];
   int x;
   int i;

   printf("Enter a string containing the number '9': ");
   scanf("%s", string);

   x = 0;
   while ( (string[x] != '9') && (x < strlen(string)) )
        x=x+1;

   if (x == strlen(string))
   {
      printf("Number '9' not found.\n");
   }
   else
   {
      printf("Number '9' located.\n");
      printf("%s\n", string);
      for (i=0; i<x; i++)
          printf(" ");

      printf("^\n");
   }

   return 0;
}
```

Find the digit 9 — points to the `while` line

Display the caret in the appropriate location — points to the `for` line

IN SIMPLE TERMS

Listing 7.9 works much like Listing 7.8. The difference is that this version of the program uses a **while** loop to locate the substring. After the user enters a string, the loop counter **x** is initialized to **0** to ensure that the program gets into the **while** loop. The loop's control expression uses the logical AND operator **&&** to make two comparisons. In the first comparison, the statement **(string[x] != '9')** checks for the substring within the string. The second comparison, **(x < strlen(string))**, ensures that the loop won't continue beyond the length of the string, which would happen if the user did not enter the number **9**.

When the while loop ends, the variable x contains the location of the substring if the string was found or the length of string if the substring wasn't found. The results of the search are printed using similar code to that found in Listing 7.8.

Listing 7.10. LOOPDEM3.C uses a *do–while* loop to locate a substring

```
#include <stdio.h>

int main()
{
    char string[255];
    int x;
    int i;

    printf("Enter a string containing the number '9': ");
    scanf("%s", string);
```

continues

157

Listing 7.10. Continued

```
                        x = 0;
                        do
                            x++;
Find the digit 9 ———— while ( (string[x] != '9') && (x < strlen(string)) );

                        if (x == strlen(string))
                        {
                            printf("Number '9' not found.\n");
                        }
                        else
                        {
                            printf("Number '9' located.\n");
Display the caret        printf("%s\n", string);
in the appropriate ———— for (i=0; i<x; i++)
location                     printf(" ");

                            printf("^\n");
                        }

                        return 0;
                    }
```

**IN SIMPLE
TERMS**

Listing 7.10 works much like Listing 7.9, except that Listing 7.10 uses a **do–while** loop rather than a **while** loop to search through the user's string. In this final version of the program, the loop continues until the substring is found or until the loop counter **x** is equal to the length of the string the user entered. In the latter case, the substring is not in the string, so an error message is printed. Otherwise, the user's string is displayed and the location of the substring is marked.

The program output for Listings 7.8, 7.9, or 7.10 looks like this:

```
c:\crook>
c:\crook>loopdem1
Enter a string containing the number '9': 1239456
Number '9' located.
1239456
    ^

c:\crook>
```

Common Rookie Mistakes

Using the wrong type of loop. As mentioned previously, each type of looping construct works best in different circumstances. For example, a `for` loop should be used only for loops that always execute from the starting limit to the ending limit. If you find yourself trying to get out of a `for` loop before the loop has run its course, you should probably be using a `while` loop or `do-while` loop.

Changing the value of a loop-control variable within the loop. The value of a `for` loop's loop-control variable should never be changed directly by your code. Except in rare circumstances, `for` loops should always be allowed to run their full cycle. If a loop is not working the way you expect it to, make sure you're not accidentally changing a loop-control variable in your code.

Faulty logic in a control expression. Just like the expressions used in `if` statements, the control expressions used in `while` and `do-while` loops can be built using the logical operators AND (`&&`), OR (`¦¦`), and NOT (`!=`). However, the more complex a control expression becomes, the more likely it is that the expression doesn't mean what you think it means. Try to keep loop-control expressions as simple as possible, and study them carefully to be sure they represent the logic you want.

Forgetting to initialize a loop-control variable in a `while` loop. Remember that a `while` loop will execute only if the control expression evaluates to true. In other words, a `while` loop's control expression should almost always evaluate to false the first time through the loop. The only exception is when the `while` loop is designed not to execute under certain circumstances.

Not incrementing the control variable correctly. If the control variable is not incremented correctly, a loop can carry on forever. This condition is known as an *infinite loop*, and it can cause programmers mental problems. If a program does not increment the control variable and test it correctly, the program may end up executing the loop forever rather than just the desired number of times.

Summing Up

▼ Repetitive operations in a computer program can be handled efficiently by program loops, including `for` loops, `while` loops, and `do—while` loops.

▼ A `for` loop instructs a program to execute a block of commands a given number of times. In the loop `for (x=0; x<10; x=x+1)`, the variable x is the loop's control variable. The x=0 clause is the initialization section, x<10 is the condition, and x=x+1 is the increment clause.

▼ By changing the increment clause in a `for` loop, you can make the loop-control variable count up or down in any increment or decrement. For example, the loop `for (x=20; x>=10; x=x-2)` counts backward by two, from 20 to 10.

▼ You can use a numeric variable for either loop limit in a `for` loop.

▼ A while loop repeats until its loop-control expression evaluates to true. The control expression can be any boolean expression (one that evaluates to true or false). These are the same kind of expressions you used with if statements.

▼ A do—while loop always executes at least once because its control expression is at the bottom of the loop rather than at the top.

In the next chapter you will learn how to use loops with a new type of data structure called an array. You will find that loops become even more powerful when they are used in conjunction with this powerful new type of program statement. In the meantime, you deserve a break. We have covered some important material in this chapter. Therefore, go ahead and get yourself an ice cold beverage from the refrigerator. See you in the next chapter.

CHAPTER 8

Powerful Structures

(Building a Better Beast)

IN A NUTSHELL

▼ Learning about arrays
▼ Using arrays with loops
▼ Understanding numerical and string arrays
▼ Initializing arrays

As you've learned by now, using variables makes your programs flexible. Thanks to variables, you can conveniently store data in your programs and retrieve it by name. You can also get input from your program's user. The best thing about variables is that they can constantly change value. They're called variables, after all, because they're variable!

Until now, you've learned about various types of numerical variables, including integers, long integers, single-precision floating-point variables, and double-precision floating-point variables. You also know about string variables, which can hold text. Now that you have a good understanding of these data types, it's time to explore one last data type—a handy data structure called an array.

An Introduction to Arrays

(A clever solution to a tricky problem)

Often in your programs, you'll want to store many values that are related in some way. Suppose you manage a bowling league and you want to keep track of each player's average. One way to do this is to give each player a variable in your program, as shown in Listing 8.1.

Listing 8.1. BOWLING1.C stores bowling averages for four bowlers

```
#include <stdio.h>

int main()
{
    int avg1, avg2, avg3, avg4;        Four different variables are required
                                       to store the bowlers' averages

    printf("Enter Fred's average: ");
    scanf("%d", &avg1);
```

```
    printf("Enter Mary's average: ");
    scanf("%d", &avg2);

    printf("Enter Thomas's average: ");
    scanf("%d", &avg3);

    printf("Enter Alice's average: ");
    scanf("%d", &avg4);

    printf("\n\nBOWLERS' AVERAGES\n");
    printf("----------------\n");
    printf("Fred: %d\n", avg1);
    printf("Mary: %d\n", avg2);
    printf("Thomas: %d\n", avg3);
    printf("Alice: %d\n", avg4);

    return 0;
}
```

IN SIMPLE TERMS

Listing 8.1 uses four **printf()** and four **scanf()** function calls to get bowling averages for four bowlers. These averages are stored in the variables **avg1**, **avg2**, **avg3**, and **avg4**. After the user inputs the averages, the program displays them along with each bowler's name.

When you run Listing 8.1, you're asked to enter bowling averages for each of four bowlers. After you enter these averages, they're displayed on-screen:

```
c:\crook>bowling1
Enter Fred's average: 140
Enter Mary's average: 154
Enter Thomas's average: 207
Enter Alice's average: 125
```

```
BOWLERS' AVERAGES
-----------------
Fred: 140
Mary: 154
Thomas: 207
Alice: 125

c:\crook>
```

Nothing too tricky going on here, right?

Now examine the listing. Remember in the last chapter when you learned to keep an eye out for repetitive program code? How about all those `printf()` and `scanf()` statements in Listing 8.1? The only real difference between them is the name of the variable used to store the input value. If you could find some way to make a loop out of this code, you'd need only one `scanf()` line to input all the data and only one `printf()` line to display the averages for all four bowlers. You could, in fact, use a `for` loop that counts from 1 to 4.

But how can you use a loop when you're stuck with four different variables? The answer is an array. An *array* is a variable that can hold more than one value. When you first studied variables, you learned that a variable is like a box in memory that holds a single value. Now, if you take a bunch of these boxes and put them together, what do you have? (No, the answer isn't "a bunch of variables smooshed together.") You have an array. For example, to store the bowling averages for your four bowlers, you'd need an array that can hold four values. You could call this array `avg`. You could also call this array `the_bowlers'_averages`, but who wants to do all that typing?

PLAY BALL!

BUZZWORD

Array
An *array* is a list of variables of the same type. All variables in an array have a common name.

Now you have an array called `avg` that can hold four bowling averages. But how can you retrieve each individual average from the array? You could run out on your front lawn in your skivvies, wave a plucked chicken over your head, and shout praises to the gods of computing. However, an easier way—and one that doesn't amuse the neighbors quite so much—is to add something called a subscript to the array's name.

A *subscript* is a number that identifies the box in which an array value is stored. For example, to refer to the first average in your `avg` array, you'd write `avg[0]`. The subscript is the number in parentheses. In this case, you're referring to the first average in the array (array subscripts always start from zero). To refer to the second average, you'd write `avg[1]`. The third and fourth averages are `avg[2]` and `avg[3]`. Get the idea?

PLAY BALL!

BUZZWORD

Subscript
A *subscript* is the number in brackets after an array's name. The subscript identifies which value in the array you want to access. For example, in the array named **numbers[10]**, the subscript is **10**, which refers to the eleventh value (because you always start counting from zero) in the array **numbers[]**.

If you're a little confused, look at Fig. 1, which shows how the `avg[]` array might look in memory. In this case, the four bowling averages are 145, 192, 160, and 203. The value of `avg[0]` is 145, the value of `avg[1]` is 192, the value of `avg[2]` is 160, and the value of `avg[3]` is 203.

C FOR ROOKIES

Fig. 1

avg(0)	145
avg(1)	192
avg(2)	160
avg(3)	203

Using a Variable as a Subscript

(The old indirect approach)

As you learned in a previous chapter, most numerical constants in a C program can be replaced by numerical variables. Suppose you were to use the variable x as the subscript for the array avg[]. Then (based on the averages in Fig. 1) if the value of x is 2, the value of avg[x] is **160**. If the value of x is 3, the value of avg[x] is **203**.

Now take one last gigantic intuitive leap (c'mon, you can do it) and think about using your subscript variable x as both the control variable in a for loop and the subscript for the avg[] array. If you use a for loop that counts from 0 to 3, you can use a single scanf() line to get the averages for all four players. Listing 8.2 shows how this is done.

> Listing 8.2. BOWLING2.C uses an array to store bowling averages for four bowlers

```
#include <stdio.h>

int main()
{
    int avg[4];                         A single array can
    int x;                              hold all the averages

    for (x=0; x<=3; x++)
    {
```

```
    printf("Enter bowler's average: ");
    scanf("%d", &avg[x]);
}

printf("\n");
                                        This loop counts from 0 to
                                        3, incrementing by one
for (x=0; x<=3; x++)
    printf("Average for bowler %d is %d\n", x+1, avg[x]);

return 0;
}
```

IN SIMPLE TERMS

Listing 8.2 creates a four-element array. The first **for** loop retrieves four averages from the user and stores them in the integer array **avg[]**. The second **for** loop displays the averages.

Here is this program's output:

```
c:\crook>bowling2
Enter bowler's average: 146
Enter bowler's average: 192
Enter bowler's average: 156
Enter bowler's average: 137

Average for bowler 1 is 146
Average for bowler 2 is 192
Average for bowler 3 is 156
Average for bowler 4 is 137

c:\crook>
```

At the beginning of Listing 8.2, you'll see a strange new variable declaration, `int avg[4]`. This tells C how large the array should be and what

type of variable the array should hold. The `int` part tells C that the array is to hold integer values. The `avg[4]` part tells C that the array is to be named `avg` and that it needs to store four integer values.

CAUTION

When you declare your arrays, make sure you have enough room for the data you have to store. Once you dimension an array, C will not allow you to store or retrieve values beyond the end of the array. For example, if you create an array as **numbers[10]** and then try to access **numbers[11]**, your program will come to a crashing halt. However, don't make your arrays bigger than they have to be because this wastes your computer's memory.

Do you understand how the program works? In the first `for` loop, the variable x starts with a value of `0`. The value retrieved by the `scanf()` statement is stored in `avg[x]`, which means that when x equals 1, the value is stored in `avg[1]`. The next time through the loop, x equals 2, so the value retrieved by the `scanf()` statement is stored in `avg[2]`. This continues until x becomes 3 and the `for` loop ends. The second `for` loop works similarly, incrementing x from `0` to `3` and printing the contents of the array one element at a time.

BUZZWORD

Elements

The memory locations that make up an array are called *elements* of the array. For example, in an array named **numbers[]**, **numbers[0]** is the first element of the array, **numbers[1]** is the second element, and so on. The reason **numbers[0]** is the first element of the array is because of the number 0 inside the subscript. It is the number inside the subscript that defines which array location is being referred to.

String Arrays

(Yet another fantabulous example of programming prowess)

Listing 8.2 shows how handy arrays can be, but there's something missing from the program. First, there's no built-in Super Mario Brothers game, so using this program for long periods of time is not only *not* exciting but also downright boring. More to the point, though, the names of the bowlers are missing. In this version of the program, you've resorted to using a number identifying the bowler rather than the name of each bowler. By creating an array to hold strings, however, you can get around this problem easily. (You can get over the Super Mario Brothers problem by taking a Nintendo break.) Listing 8.3 shows how this is done.

> ### Listing 8.3. BOWLING3.C uses an array for the names and averages of the bowlers

```
#include <stdio.h>

int main()
{
    int avg[4];
    char name[4][255];                    A string array can hold all the
    int x;                                names of the bowlers

    for (x=0; x<=3; x++)
    {
        printf("Enter bowler's name: ");
        scanf("%s", &name[x]);            The subscript x
                                          accesses both
                                          arrays and
        printf("Enter bowler's average: ");  thus matches
        scanf("%d", &avg[x]);             the names of
    }                                     the bowlers
                                          with their
    printf("\n");                         averages
```

continues

Listing 8.3. Continued

```
printf("\n\nBOWLERS' AVERAGES\n");
printf("----------------\n");

for (x=0; x<=3; x++)
    printf("Average for %s is %d\n", name[x], avg[x]);

return 0;
}
```

IN SIMPLE TERMS

Listing 8.3 creates two four-element arrays, one for integers and one for strings. The first **for** loop retrieves four names and averages from the user and stores them in the arrays **name[]** and **avg[]**. The second **for** loop displays the names and averages.

The output looks like this:

```
c:\crook>bowling3
Enter bowler's name: Fred
Enter bowler's average: 156
Enter bowler's name: Mary
Enter bowler's average: 176
Enter bowler's name: Thomas
Enter bowler's average: 135
Enter bowler's name: Alice
Enter bowler's average: 185
```

```
BOWLERS' AVERAGES
-----------------
Average for Fred is 156
Average for Mary is 176
Average for Thomas is 135
Average for Alice is 185


c:\crook>
```

When you run Listing 8.3, you're asked to enter not only the averages of the bowlers but also their names. The names are stored in a string array, and the averages are stored in an integer array. Because both arrays use the same subscript value for each bowler's name and average, the first name in the string array matches the first average in the integer array, the second name matches the second average, and so on. You then can simply use another loop to print the names and averages.

You probably notice something different about the declaration for the string array. It looks like this:

```
char name[4][255];
```

The first number in brackets is the number of strings available in the array. The second number refers to the maximum length of each string inside the array.

If you remember the discussion of strings in Chapter 5, "Working with Text," you probably notice something similar between arrays and string variables. If you already noticed this, you get bonus points. The reason for the similarity is that a string actually is an array of characters. Therefore, a string array is an array of character arrays, which is why the program must specify two numbers when declaring the string array (see Fig. 2). Notice, however, that when referring to the string later in the program, the program only refers to the element in the string array that is being referred to.

C FOR ROOKIES

Fig. 2

string[0]	string[1]	string[2]	string[3]

string name
number of strings
char string [4][8]; maximum length of strings
character keyword

Initializing Arrays

(Starting off right)

Your bowling averages program still isn't as efficient as it could be. Why, for example, should you have to enter the name of each bowler every time you run the program? Do you really need that much typing practice? In most cases, the names of the bowlers won't change. There must be some way to store data in your programs without having to enter it from the keyboard. You could get a grease pencil, write the bowlers' names on your computer's screen, and hope they sink in. But a better (and more dependable) method is to initialize the array when it is first declared.

To assign an initial value to an array, use the following array declaration:

```
int avg[4] = {123, 456, 789, 159};
```

or without specifying the size, use

```
int avg[] = {123, 456, 789, 159};
```

174

The above two declarations have the exact same result. In the second case, C counts the number of elements you have declared and forces the array to be the appropriate size. In the first case, you could specify an array with a larger size and then only initialize the first several elements. The easiest method is the second method, because it forces the C compiler to do the dirty work of counting the number of elements inside an array. However, there certainly are not going to be any programming police standing by your computer telling you which way to declare your arrays. One method is not any better than the other.

To initialize a string variable, use the following array declaration:

```
char name[4][255] = {"first", "second", "third", "fourth"};
```

In this case, the two numbers are required. The reason is that when the compiler looks at the list of string array elements, it has a harder time counting them. Since it cannot handle this type of counting, it is up to the programmer to do so.

Listing 8.4 shows how pre-initialized arrays work. It's important that you understand this program because this is a common method of creating initialized data.

Listing 8.4. BOWLING4.C stores the names of bowlers in an initialized string array

The **name** array is initialized to contain four names

```
#include <stdio.h>

char name[4][255] = {"Fred", "Mary", "Thomas", "Alice"};

int main()
{
    int avg[4];
    int x;
```

continues

Listing 8.4. Continued

```c
for (x=0; x<=3; x++)
{
   printf("Enter %s's average: ", name[x]);
   scanf("%d", &avg[x]);
}

printf("\n");

printf("\n\nBOWLERS' AVERAGES\n");
printf("----------------\n");

for (x=0; x<=3; x++)
   printf("Average for %s is %d\n", name[x], avg[x]);

return 0;
}
```

IN SIMPLE TERMS

Listing 8.4 dimensions two four-element arrays, one for integers and one for strings. Then a **for** loop counts from 0 to 3 requesting the bowlers' averages from the user. The names of the bowlers are stored in the string array **name[ ]**, and their averages are stored in the integer array **avg[ ]**. The second **for** loop displays the names and averages.

This program produces the following output:

```
c:\crook>bowling4
Enter Fred's average: 165
Enter Mary's average: 134
Enter Thomas's average: 187
Enter Alice's average: 174
```

```
BOWLERS' AVERAGES
----------------
Average for Fred is 165
Average for Mary is 134
Average for Thomas is 187
Average for Alice is 174


c:\crook>
```

When you run Listing 8.4, you're no longer asked to enter each bowler's name. Instead, the names are stored in an initialized array. Each time through the first `for` loop, you're asked to provide that bowler's average. By the end of the loop, the averages of all four bowlers have been placed in the `avg[]` array.

You can pre-initialize arrays with any kind of data. You just have to be sure that you initialize each data element with the right type of data. You couldn't, for example, initialize an integer variable with string data. To see how this works, suppose you now want to include the average and name of each bowler in the program's data. Listing 8.5 is the bowling averages program with this change installed.

Listing 8.5. BOWLING5.C stores the names and averages of the bowlers in pre-initialized arrays

```
#include <stdio.h>
```

Bowlers' names ———— `char name[4][255] = {"Fred", "Mary", "Thomas", "Alice"};`
Bowlers' averages ———— `int avg[4] = {145, 192, 160, 203};`

```
int main()
{
    int x;

    printf("\n\nBOWLERS' AVERAGES\n");
    printf("----------------\n");
```

continues

Listing 8.5. Continued

```
    for (x=0; x<=3; x++)
        printf("Average for %s is %d\n", name[x], avg[x]);

    return 0;
}
```

IN SIMPLE TERMS

Listing 8.5 dimensions two four-element arrays, one is for integers and the other is for strings. It sets their beginning values in the array declaration. A **for** loop counts from 0 to 3 and displays the names and averages of each bowler.

Here is the output for this program:

```
c:\crook>bowling5


BOWLERS' AVERAGES
----------------
Average for Fred is 145
Average for Mary is 192
Average for Thomas is 160
Average for Alice is 203

c:\crook>
```

Listing 8.5 is similar to Listing 8.4. The main difference is that you no longer have to enter data from the keyboard. All the data is contained in the program's array initialization section. If a bowler's average changes, you have to change only the appropriate entry in the program.

Common Rookie Mistakes

Allowing array subscripts to go out of bounds. It's easier than you might think—especially when you use `while` or `do-while` loops—to allow an array's subscript to get larger (or smaller) than the array can handle. Once you've dimensioned an array, you can never access an array element beyond the end of the array. If you do, your program will crash (come to an abrupt halt).

All arrays start with the subscript of 0. When an array is declared with a statement like `int x[4]`, it declares an integer array that has four elements. The first element of the array is referred to as `x[0]`, the second element is referred to as `x[1]`, the third element as `x[2]`, and the fourth element as `x[3]`. The array subscript is always one less than the actual element because array subscripts begin counting from zero.

Summing Up

▼ Arrays enable you to store many values under a single variable name.

▼ An array's subscript, which is a number within parentheses appended to the array's name, identifies each element of the array.

▼ The subscripts within an array always start at zero and go up. Therefore, if an array named `arr` is declared to be three elements long, the first element is `arr[0]`, the second element is `arr[1]`, and the last element is `arr[2]`.

▼ By using a numerical variable for an array's subscript, you can easily access each element of the array within a loop.

▼ To tell C how large an array should be, you must declare the array by following the array name with brackets ([and]), which are enclosed by a number that tells the maximum number of elements the array can hold.

You now know most of the basics of programming in C—everything you have to know to produce useful and powerful programs. Before you go on your way, however, you need to learn modular programming. This important topic is covered in the final chapter.

CHAPTER 9

Modular Programming
(Tying up Some Loose Ends)

IN A NUTSHELL

- ▼ Writing modular programs
- ▼ Designing programs from the top down
- ▼ Writing sub-routines and functions

Until now, your programs have been pretty short, each designed to demonstrate a single programming technique. When you start writing real programs, however, you'll quickly discover that they can grow to many pages of code. When programs get long, they also get harder to organize and read. To overcome this problem, professional programmers developed something called modular programming, one topic you study in this chapter.

The Top-Down Approach to Programming

(A programmer's pyramid plan)

Like I said, long programs are hard to organize and read. A full-length program contains many pages of code, and trying to find a specific part of the program in all that code can be tough. You can use modular program-design techniques to solve this problem. Using modular programming techniques, you can break a long program into individual modules, each of which performs a specific task.

To understand how modular programming works, consider how you might organize the cleaning of a house. (The only reasonable way to clean my house is to douse it with gasoline and throw in a lighted match, but we won't get into that now.) The main task might be called CLEAN HOUSE. Thinking about cleaning an entire house, however, can be overwhelming—just ask my wife. So, to make the task easier, you can break it down into a number of smaller steps. These steps might be CLEAN LIVING ROOM, CLEAN BEDROOM, CLEAN KITCHEN, and CLEAN BATHROOM.

After breaking the housecleaning task down into room-by-room steps, you have a better idea of what to do. But cleaning a room is also a pretty big task—especially if it hasn't been done in a while. So why not break each room a step down, too? For example, cleaning the living room

could be broken down into PICK UP ROOM, DUST AND POLISH, CLEAN FURNITURE, and VACUUM RUG. After breaking each room's cleaning down into steps, your housecleaning job is organized much like a pyramid, with the general task on the top. As you work your way down the pyramid, from the main task to the room-by-room list and finally to the tasks for each room, the tasks get more and more specific.

Of course, when cleaning a house, you don't usually write a list of steps. If you're an efficient housecleaner, the steps are organized in your mind. (If you clean house like me, there are only two steps: TURN ON TV and COLLAPSE ON COUCH.) However, when writing a program, which is a more conceptual task, you may not have a clear idea of exactly what needs to be done. This can lead to your being overwhelmed by the project. Overwhelmed programmers are easy to spot. They stare at their computer screens blankly and often break into bouts of weeping.

Breaking programming tasks down into steps, or modules, is called *modular programming*. And when you break your program's modules down into even smaller modules—as we did with the task of cleaning a house—you're using a top-down approach to program design. By using top-down programming techniques, you can write any program as a series of small, easy-to-handle tasks.

C provides two types of modules that you can use when writing programs. The first, subroutines, is covered in the next section. The second, functions, is covered later in this chapter.

Using Subroutines

(Blocks in the pyramid)

One type of program module is a subroutine. A *subroutine* is like a small program within your main program. If you write a housecleaning

program, the subroutines in the main module might be called
`CleanLivingRoom`, `CleanBedroom`, `CleanKitchen`, and `CleanBathroom`.
The `CleanLivingRoom` subroutine would contain all the steps needed to
clean the living room, the `CleanBedroom` subroutine would contain all
the steps needed to clean a bedroom, and so on.

Of course, it takes an extremely talented programmer to get a computer
to clean a house. (If you manage that trick, contact me immediately.)
We need a more computer-oriented example. Suppose you want to write
a program that displays instructions on-screen.

Listing 9.1. SUBRTN1.C displays instructions for a game

```c
#include <stdio.h>

int main()
{
    DisplayInstructions();              Subroutine call

    return 0;
}


void DisplayInstructions()
{
    printf("Guess a Number Game\n");
    printf("\n\n");
    printf("Try to guess the number I\n");
    printf("am thinking of.  The number\n");
    printf("will be between 0 and 100.\n\n");   Subroutine body
    printf("You have an\n");
    printf("unlimited number of tries.\n\n");
    printf("Good Luck\n\n");

}
```

Listing 9.1 calls the subroutine **DisplayInstructions**. In the subroutine, the program uses the **printf()** function to display information on-screen.

Here is the output from Listing 9.1:

```
c:\crook>subrtn1
Guess a Number Game


Try to guess the number I
am thinking of.  The number
will be between 0 and 100.

You have an
unlimited number of tries.

Good Luck


c:\crook>
```

Now for the million dollar question: How does this program work? The program is divided into two modules. The first is the main program, which comprises the section of code inside the curly braces for `main()`. This module is called the main program because it is at the highest level of your top-down design. That is, no other module uses the main program, but the main program calls modules that are lower in level.

The second module in Listing 9.1 is the `DisplayInstructions` subroutine. This subroutine is called by the main program, so the `DisplayInstructions` subroutine is considered to be one level down from the main program in the top-down design.

There are two parts to using subroutines inside a program. The first part is calling the subroutine. In Listing 9.1, the subroutine is called like this:

```
DisplayInstructions();
```

Notice the ending semicolon. The second part to using a subroutine is declaring it. The declaration looks like this:

```
void DisplayInstructions()
{
    printf("Guess a Number Game\n");
    printf("\n\n");
    printf("Try to guess the number I\n");
    printf("am thinking of.  The number\n");
    printf("will be between 0 and 100.\n\n");
    printf("You have an\n");
    printf("unlimited number of tries.\n\n");
    printf("Good Luck\n\n");

}
```

Notice the word `void` at the very beginning of the subroutine. This portion of the subroutine indicates that the routine returns no value. This keyword, followed by the subroutine name and up to the end of the parenthesis is how C tells that you are creating a subroutine. The lines of code between curly braces are the body of the subroutine.

You can also pass arguments to a subroutine. These arguments can be used inside the subroutine. To declare an argument inside the subroutine, you must tell C how many arguments there are and what type of data is passed in the arguments. The number of arguments are declared by listing them after the function call declaration. For example, you could use the statement

```
void DisplayInstructions(argument1, argument2)
```

to tell C that you are going to pass two arguments. To tell C what type of arguments you are going to pass, you must declare them immediately after the function declaration but before the curly braces. For example:

```
void DisplayInstructions(argument1, argument2)
int argument1;
float argument2;
{
...
}
```

NOTE

A subroutine can have as many arguments as you like, but you must be sure that the arguments you specify in the subroutine's call match the arguments in the subroutine's declaration.

That wasn't too tough, was it? Unfortunately, using subroutines is a little more complicated than it may appear from the above discussion. If you jump right in and try to write your own subroutines at this point, you'll run into trouble faster than a dog catches fleas in the spring. Before you can write good subroutines, you must at least learn about something called variable scope. Coincidentally, variable scope is the next topic in this chapter.

Variable Scope

(Help for variables with bad breath)

Now that you know a little about subroutines, you should know how C organizes variables between modules.

You need arguments in your subroutines because of something called *variable scope*, which determines whether program modules can "see" a specific variable.

A variable in one module is not accessible in another (unless it's shared, which you'll learn about in a minute). So, when you don't explicitly pass x as an argument, other subroutines can't access it. This type of variable is known as a *local variable*.

A variable that is accessible by more than one module is called a *global variable*.

BUZZWORD

Local Variables/Global Variables

Local variables are those variables not accessible outside of the module in which they appear. *Global variables*, on the other hand, are accessible anywhere within a program. It is the variable scope which determines whether program modules can have access to specific variables.

By not allowing a variable to be seen outside of the module in which it's used, you never have to worry about some other module accidentally changing that variable's value. Moreover, local variables make subroutines self-contained modules, as if everything the subroutine needs were put together in a little box. If the value of a variable used in a subroutine is giving your program trouble, you know exactly which module to check. You don't need to search your entire program to find the problem any more than you need to search your entire house to find a quart of milk.

The opposite of a local variable is a global variable. Global variables can be used in any module anywhere in your program. Listing 9.2 is a program that makes use of local and global variables.

Listing 9.2. SUBRTN2.C uses a global variable

```c
#include <stdio.h>

int global;

void main()
{
    int local;

    local = 5;
    global = 5;

    printf("Before calling Subroutine()\n");
    printf("local = %d\n", local);
    printf("global = %d\n\n", global);

    Subroutine(8);

    printf("After calling Subroutine()\n");
    printf("local = %d\n", local);
    printf("global = %d\n\n", global);

}


void Subroutine(passed)
int passed;
{
    int local;

    local = 10;
    global = 10;

    printf("Inside subroutine\n");

    printf("local = %d\n", local);
    printf("global = %d\n\n", global);

}
```

Global variables are declared outside of any other modules

Local variables are declared inside a module

Local variables are declared inside a module

OK

CHAPTER 9

C FOR ROOKIES

IN SIMPLE TERMS

Listing 9.2 creates several variables. One variable is named **global** and is declared outside of any functions. The other variable is named **local**. Two different instances of **local** are created, one inside **main()** and the other inside **Subroutine()**. The **printf()** function is used to display the value of the variables at different points within the program.

Here is the output from Listing 9.2:

```
c:\crook>subrtn2
Before calling Subroutine()
local = 5
global = 5

Inside subroutine
local = 10
global = 10

After calling Subroutine()
local = 5
global = 10


c:\crook>
```

TIP

As a novice programmer, you may think that using global variables is a great programming shortcut. After all, if you make all your variables global, you'll never have to worry about passing arguments to subroutines. However, a program with a lot of global variables is a poorly designed program—hard to read and hard to debug. You should write your programs to include as few global variables as possible.

190

Using Functions

(Still more blocks in the pyramid)

Functions are the main way you can break up your programs into modules. But unlike subroutines, functions always return a value to the main program. You've used C functions before in this book. The `strlen()` function is one. The value it returns is the number of characters in a string.

In fact, subroutines are actually just a type of function. If you look through boring technical magazines, there is no reference to subroutines inside C programs. Instead, there are only functions that don't return a value. This train of thought is a little different from other languages, such as Pascal and BASIC.

You write functions much like subroutines. However, function calls can assign the function's return value to a variable. Suppose you have a function named `GetNum()` that gets a number from the user and returns it to your program. A call to the function might look something like `num = GetNum()`.

Listing 9.3 is a short program that illustrates how to use functions in your C programs.

Listing 9.3. FUNCTION.C includes a function module

```c
#include <stdio.h>

int main()
{
   printf("You typed the number %d\n", GetInput());

   return 0;
}
```

└─ This is a function call

continues

C FOR ROOKIES

Listing 9.3. Continued

This tells what
type of value the ——— int GetInput()
function returns

```
int GetInput()
{
    int value;

    printf("Please enter a number : ");
    scanf("%d", &value);

    return value;
}
```

This is the
function body

**IN SIMPLE
TERMS**

The main program in Listing 9.3 calls the function **GetInput()**
to get a number from the user. This number is stored in the
variable **value.** After getting the number, the main program
uses **printf()** to display the string the user typed.

The function GetInput() allows the user to enter a number. The
scanf() statement retrieves the number from the user, after which the
number is returned by the function.

Here is the output from Listing 9.3:

```
c:\crook>function
Please enter a number : 999
You typed the number 999

c:\crook>
```

When you run Listing 9.3, the program prompts you to enter a number. Then, the program shows you what you typed, just in case you forget what it was—or maybe just to verify that the function did indeed return the string to the main program.

Look at the main program first. Notice the call to `GetInput()` is actually part of the `printf()` statement, as follows:

```
printf("You typed the number %d\n", GetInput());
```

Then, the function is actually found later in the program, as follows:

```
int GetInput()
{
   int value;

   printf("Please enter a number : ");
   scanf("%d", &value);

   return value;
}
```

The first word declares what type of value the function should return. In this case, it is an `int` or an integer value. The function then declares a local variable, `value`. The `printf()` function is used to display a prompt to the user, and then `scanf()` is used to input the value from the user. Finally, the line `return value;` is used to return the variable `value` to the main program.

This shows some of the differences between subroutines and functions. Subroutines always start with the keyword `void`, whereas functions start with the keyword `int`, `char`, `float` or whatever type of return value. Also, because subroutines don't return any type of value, they don't have a `return` statement.

As you can see, functions are similar to subroutines. In fact, you can pass arguments to functions the same way you do subroutines. Just add parentheses to the function's name and list the arguments, separated by commas, inside the parentheses. Don't forget to match the arguments in the function's call with those in the function's declaration.

Now, you've come to the part of the book that separates the men from the boys, the women from the girls, and the butterflies from the caterpillars. Are you ready? Because it's time to take a look at...

...The Final Program

(One last spin around the block)

Listing 9.4, the last program in this book, is an example of how to design a modular program. It also summarizes much of what you've learned in this book.

Listing 9.4. GUESS.C is a number guessing game

```c
#include <stdio.h>

int main()
{
    int score;

    DisplayInstructions();
    score = PlayGame();
    ShowScore(score);

    return 0;
}
```

This is the main module

```
/*****************************/
void DisplayInstructions()
{
    printf("Guess a Number Game\n");
    printf("\n\n");
    printf("Try to guess the number I\n");
    printf("am thinking of.  The number\n");
    printf("will be between 0 and 100.\n\n");
    printf("You have an\n");
    printf("unlimited number of tries.\n\n");
    printf("Good Luck\n\n");

}

/*****************************/
int PlayGame()
{
    int number, guess, count;

    guess = 0;
    count = 0;

    /* make sure the number is between 100 */
    while ((number >= 100) || (number <0) )
        number = rand();

    while (guess != number)
    {
        printf("Guess the number I am thinking of :");
        scanf("%d", &guess);

        count = count + 1;

        if (guess == number)
        {
            printf("You guessed it!\n");
```

These are comments

Continue looping while the guess is not equal to the number

continues

195

C FOR ROOKIES

Listing 9.4. Continued

```c
        return count;
    }
    else if (guess < number)
    {
        printf("Your guess is too low.  Try again.\n");
    }
    else if (guess > number)
    {
        printf("Your guess is too high. Try again.\n");
    }
    }

}


/****************************/
void ShowScore(score)
int score;
{
    printf("You took %d tries.\n", score);

}
```

When you run Listing 9.4, it carries on a number guessing game with you, as follows:

```
c:\crook>guess
Guess a Number Game


Try to guess the number I
am thinking of.  The number
will be between 0 and 100.

You have an
unlimited number of tries.
```

C FOR ROOKIES

CHAPTER 9

```
Good Luck

Guess the number I am thinking of :50
Your guess is too high. Try again.
Guess the number I am thinking of :25
Your guess is too high. Try again.
Guess the number I am thinking of :15
Your guess is too low.  Try again.
Guess the number I am thinking of :20
Your guess is too high. Try again.
Guess the number I am thinking of :18
Your guess is too high. Try again.
Guess the number I am thinking of :19
Your guess is too high. Try again.
Guess the number I am thinking of :16
You guessed it!
You took 7 tries.


c:\crook>
```

The program creates a random number between 0 and 100 that it instructs you to guess.

Because of the size of Listing 9.4, there's no "In Simple Terms" box describing how it works. In a way, this program is your final exam. Go through it line by line, figuring out how it does what it does. Analyzing programs is a skill you need to develop if you plan to continue in programming.

Before you get started, there are a few things in Listing 9.4 you haven't seen before. First, within the PlayGame() function, the rand() function returns a random number. This random number is actually a pseudo-random number. What this means is that the number is not really random (talk about a contradiction of terms). Random numbers in a computer are not truly random, but are instead calculated by a formula. Some C compilers allow you to enter a new value that the formula is calculated on, thereby creating the illusion of a random number. However, the Personal C Compiler does not have this capability.

In the main program, notice that some lines start with /* and end with */. These are comments. You can use comments to document your program, like leaving notes to yourself (or whoever ends up reading your program) to explain what the program does. When C sees these symbols, it knows that the text in between them is a comment and ignores it. If you want, you can have an entire block of lines that are nothing but comments. C won't even care if you put a letter to Uncle Henry in the middle of your program, as long as it's within the /* and */ characters.

Everything else in Listing 9.4 should be familiar to you. If you have trouble figuring out a section of the code, try to think like a computer, taking the program a line at a time, making sure you know what each line does. If you do, you'll have no trouble figuring out the entire program.

Common Rookie Mistakes

Writing lengthy modules. Programs are broken up into small modules to make program code easier to understand. To this end, each module in a program should perform only a single task so that it stays short and to the point. When you try to cram too much functionality into a module, it loses its identity. If you can't state a module's purpose in two or three words, it's probably doing too much.

Confusing local and global variables. Remember that if you haven't declared a variable outside of other modules, it is accessible only in the module in which it appears. This means that you can have two or more variables with the same name in a program, all holding different values. Use arguments to pass variables between modules. Use global variables only when unavoidable.

Confusing subroutines and functions. If you need to return a value from a module, use a function. If you're not returning a value, use a subroutine.

Mixing up the order of arguments. You can pass one or more arguments to subroutines and functions. However, keep in mind that the arguments are passed to the module in the order in which they appear in the module call. The module's declaration lists the arguments in the same order they are listed in the module call.

Summing Up

▼ Modular programming means breaking up a program into a series of simple tasks.

▼ Top-down programming means organizing modules in a hierarchy, with general-purpose modules at the top that call specific-purpose modules lower in the hierarchy. A program written this way can be thought of as a pyramid, with the main program at the top. The further down the pyramid you go, the more specific in function the modules become.

▼ Subroutines and functions are the two types of modules you can use when writing a C program. Functions must return values, whereas subroutines do not. Subroutines are, in fact, a type of function.

▼ Local variables are accessible only within the module in which they appear. Global variables are accessible anywhere in a program.

▼ To get random numbers, use the rand() function to return a random number.

Always More to Learn

(Groan)

You've now reached the end of *C for Rookies*. (Stop cheering, please.) If you've read each lesson carefully, you should have a good idea of what computer programming is all about. But there's much more you need to know if you want to pursue programming as a profession or even as a serious hobby. Don't stop your studies with this book. Two books you might want to check out are *Do It Yourself Turbo* C++ (Sams Publishing) or *Crash Course in* C (Que), both by yours truly. Either of these texts will provide excellent training in more advanced C programming.

Regardless of where your studies lead you, there is nothing more important when learning a new skill than practice. Reading a book is only the first step. To really understand the art of programming, you must program—a lot. The more programs you design and write, the better programmer you'll become. Don't be afraid to experiment with your programs. There's nothing you can do with C that will damage your machine. If you're willing to put in the time and effort, you'll soon amaze yourself and your friends with the wonderful things you can make your computer do.

Index

Symbols

A

V

variable names, 51, 102
  creating, 48
  errors, 58
variable scope, 188-190
  arguments, 188
  modules, 188-190
variables
  arrays, 164-167
  assigning, 78, 79
  averages, 165
  constants, 76
  creating
    for holding text, 52
  declaring, 75
  decrementing, 139, 145-146
  `for` loops, 146-148
  global, 188-190
  incrementing, 139, 145-146
    infinite loops, 160

  initializing, 151
  local, 188-190
  mathematical operations,
    62-65
  memory, 47-48
  numeric, 52
  `scanf()` function, 49-51
  string, 52
  subscripts, 168-170
viewing programs, 24

W-X-Y-Z

`while` loops, 148-151, 155-156
  see also boolean expressions
Whole words only option, 37
writing modules, 198